What people are saying

Radical Chains

Compelling, compact...wide-ranging...A much-needed explanation for why a return to class is essential if we are to have a future worthy of human beings.

Paul LeBlanc, author of *A Short History of the US Working Class* and *From Marx to Gramsci*

Beautifully written, *Radical Chains* shows how class struggle has put the issue of human freedom on the agenda over and over again. It is panoramic in its historical scope...a much needed challenge to the fragmentation wrought by academic postmodernism.

Tony McKenna, author of *The War on Marxism*

This important and timely book makes the argument that the side-lining of class in mainstream political debate today has only one winner: the establishment.

Holly Rigby, teacher activist and writer

Sets right the disastrous error of representing class as an identity or a cultural category equivalent to other twenty-first-century identities. An urgent read.

Rachel Holmes, author of *Eleanor Marx: A Life*

Covering a vast terrain from the necessity of organization to the problems of identity politics, this is a much-needed treatise on the emancipatory possibilities of understanding class as a social relation.

Alpa Shah, Professor of Anthropology at the London School of Economics, author of the award-winning *Nightmarch: Among India's Revolutionary Guerrillas*

This is a powerful book...It will be controversial with commentators, many academics and mainstream left politicians, but his case that the working class has always been the most important source of radical ideas in society is strong. Read it.
Raju J Das, Professor at York University, Toronto and author of *Marxist Class Theory for a Skeptical World*

This fantastic and concise global survey of class struggles... raises questions and teaches lessons that we mustn't ignore as we head into the coming storms.
Mike Wayne, author of, *England's Discontents: Political Cultures and National Identities*

A much-needed book at a time of growing class struggle, but when class still remains on the margins in the academy. A clear-sighted and accessible analysis of how to understand class in the neoliberal era.
Deepa Kumar, Professor of Media Studies, Rutgers University, author of *Outside the Box: Corporate Media, Globalization and the UPS Strike*

Also by the Author

The British State: A Warning, Zero Books,
ISBN: 978-1-78904-329-7

How the Establishment Lost Control, Zero Books,
ISBN: 978-1-78535-631-5

The People v Tony Blair, Zero Books, ISBN: 978-1-78099-816-9

Radical Chains

Why Class Matters

Radical Chains

Why Class Matters

Chris Nineham

Winchester, UK
Washington, USA

JOHN HUNT PUBLISHING

First published by Zero Books, 2023
Zero Books is an imprint of John Hunt Publishing Ltd., No. 3 East St., Alresford,
Hampshire SO24 9EE, UK
office@jhpbooks.com
www.johnhuntpublishing.com
www.zero-books.net

For distributor details and how to order please visit the 'Ordering' section on our website.

Text copyright: Chris Nineham 2022

ISBN: 978 1 78904 935 0
978 1 78904 936 7 (ebook)
Library of Congress Control Number: 2022937876

A CIP catalogue record for this book is available from the British Library.

Design: Stuart Davies

UK: Printed and bound by CPI Group (UK) Ltd, Croydon, CR0 4YY
Printed in North America by CPI GPS partners

We operate a distinctive and ethical publishing philosophy in
all areas of our business, from our global network of authors to
production and worldwide distribution.

Contents

1. Introduction: The Great Denial   1

2. A Universal Class   10

3. At Heaven's Gate   44

4. The Myth of Class Compromise   72

5. Going Underground   104

6. Conclusion: The Return of the Repressed?   139

Endnotes   165

Acknowledgements

This short book really has been a collective effort, although of course I take responsibility for its final judgements. As will become clear its argument was developed from a long and rich tradition of participating in and trying to analyse working class struggle, a process which includes countless discussions with fellow socialists. I would like to thank in particular Lindsey German, Doug Lain, John Rees, Alistair Cartwright, Des Freedman, Feyzi Ismail, Dave Randall, Dragan Plavšić, Alia Butt, Jim Aindow and Elaine Graham-Leigh for encouraging me to write it, discussing the subject and in many cases commenting on a first draft. Thanks also to Elaine Graham-Leigh, Dominic Alexander and John Romans for their thorough subbing. My gratitude as well to everyone else involved at Zero.

Ideas do not fall from heaven, and nothing comes to us in a dream.
Antonio Labriola[1]

Each decade we shiftily declare we have buried class; each decade the coffin stays empty.
Richard Hoggart[2]

Where the chains of capitalism are forged, there must the chains be broken.
Rosa Luxemburg[3]

1. Introduction: The Great Denial

Over the last four decades, as society has become more unequal than at any time since the 1920s, class has largely dropped out of mainstream discussion. As unions have been attacked, wages slashed, the welfare state ransacked and the number of billionaires has boomed, politicians, academics and commentators have lined up to announce that class is no more. The tendency reached a climax in 1999 after Tony Blair led the British Labour Party into a loving embrace with the free market and announced, 'the class war is over'.[4]

Experts have been dreaming up ways to describe the world without mentioning Karl Marx's 'two main classes' ever since the first working-class organisations emerged in the earlier part of the nineteenth century. These efforts, however, have peaked in the neoliberal years. In universities, labour-studies departments were closed and business studies flourished. Newspapers sacked their labour correspondents and focussed on stock prices instead of strike statistics. Ignoring their roots in working-class organisation, social-democratic parties everywhere dropped the rhetoric of class. Intellectuals from the right, the liberal centre and parts of the left fell over themselves to dismiss class by introducing a range of new social categories, separating class from any economic basis, reducing it to one division among many others or just denying it altogether.

Their efforts have taken many forms. One common theme is the idea that the workforce has become transient, no longer attached to particular workplaces or industries and, in one influential version, permanently precarious. Another idea is that production has become 'immaterial', creating information and services rather than goods or commodities. Other intersecting theories include the idea that the majority has become middle class or that the system is characterised by 'wasteland' populations, mainly but

1

not only in the Global South, completely excluded from the world of capitalist exploitation.[5] There is also a widespread view, often connected in various ways with the other ideas, that gender, sex, nation or race have supplanted class as the defining categories or identities in the twenty-first-century world.

On the few occasions when class is discussed, it too is often treated as an identity or a cultural category, linked to lifestyle, income and consumption rather than economic role. In the context of the massive expansion of consumer goods, this has helped to obscure or confuse real class distinctions. Commentators like to insist that the dwindling of a caricatured 'old working class' with cloth caps and overalls signifies that we are mostly all middle class. The fact that people from different walks of life sometimes wear the same brand of trainers or use the same mobile phone is presented as proof positive that we are living in a classless society where patterns of consumption trump our position in the world of work.[6]

It may seem paradoxical that class has been swept under the carpet just as inequality has surged, but there is a logic to it. Achieving a society as unequal as ours depended on defeating key bastions of working-class organisation. The reorganisation of capitalism that came to be called neoliberalism involved a concerted assault on the working class which had disastrous results for workers. Serial defeats for the working class lent credibility to the idea that workers had less social weight. The wave of new technology, plant closures and international restructuring that accompanied it appeared to give objectivity to the notion that we were dealing with a whole new social set up. And as we shall see, attacking the *idea* of class was an important element of the new class war that was unleashed by the New Right in the 1970s and 1980s. Ironically, surrender on this issue, and acceptance by parts of the left that class was no longer key, is one of the reasons why employers have achieved success in their class war.

Awkward attitudes

One group unconvinced by all this are working people themselves. Throughout the neoliberal years, an almost unchanged majority of British people have identified as working class.[7] Even in the US, where the concept has been under extreme attack, most of those earning less than $50,000 a year call themselves working class.[8] What is more, even in the darkest days of the neoliberal offensive, they have held on to many of the ideas historically associated with workers; a concern for equality, for public ownership, for trade-union rights and in general for limits to the power and wealth of big business and the rich.[9]

This book first of all puts the case that working people themselves were and are right. Far from disappearing, class divisions have deepened and the working class has in fact grown. As Marx eloquently explained in *The Communist Manifesto*, capitalism is nothing if not dynamic and fast changing. The neoliberal turn has involved traumatic transformation and reorganisation at every level of society, exactly the kind of 'constant revolutionizing of production and uninterrupted disturbance of all social conditions' that Marx wrote about.[10] New industries have replaced old, new technologies have come to dominate, world production chains have been transformed, the machinery of state has been reengineered to serve big finance and corporate power unambiguously. All this, interwoven as it has been with the brutal drive to restore profitability, has had a devastating impact on the lives of billions. It has impoverished whole communities, thrown millions out of work, plunged entire regions into crisis, created massive population flows, and slashed the standard of living of huge numbers. Much less reported is the fact that all this has coincided with the majority of the world's population becoming wage labourers for the first time in history.[11]

As with every major capitalist reorganisation, the neoliberal turn has restructured class in deep and complex ways. New production methods and opening up markets around the world have created new national and international divisions of labour. New technologies, management offensives and offshoring have driven down wages and conditions and broken up centres of working-class power. As part of this process, ruling classes have ruthlessly weaponised racial and gender divisions in new ways to divide populations and undermine resistance.

The offensive has massively weakened working-class organisation. It has hollowed out social democracy and led to a decades-long flatlining of strike action at historically low levels. The argument here is that the process as a whole has also intensified not weakened the hold of capital over the lives of the world's populations. Amongst other things it has created new centres of production, both high and low tech, in many parts of the world. One result of the internationalising of production has been a 'logistics revolution': an explosion in transport and communications that has generated massive new concentrations of networked labourers. We have to understand the massive changes that have taken place in the world system, but we can only do that effectively if we grasp that it is still a system with the exploitation of workers at its heart.

These arguments are important not just because they challenge misconceptions about the nature of the world we live in, although that would of course be reason enough to make them. They matter too because they have a bearing on the very possibility of radical resistance and of alternative ways of organising society. Class is not just important as a category for understanding capitalist society. My contention in what follows is that it is the essential basis for critiquing it and ultimately transcending it. The downgrading of class risks abandoning any attempt at a total, holistic understanding of the capitalist world and, it inevitably follows, waving goodbye to the idea that we can fight for a fundamentally different and better one.

For this reason, amongst others, this book starts by exploring

Marx and Engel's writings about class. The two nineteenth-century socialists and writers were the first to place class at the centre of a theoretical world view and a political strategy. For them class was not one division or category amongst others. It was a *social relation*, and it was the defining social relation, one that profoundly shaped the whole of society. Understanding the class nature of society for Marx was neither simply a way of describing how society worked nor a guarantee that society would evolve into socialism. What was essential for Marx even in his most technical explorations of the way capitalism functions was the way in which it produces a class that has an *interest* in overthrowing it and an ability and a tendency to comprehend that interest consciously.

Marx's insistence on the importance of class in the contemporary world was based on a desire to see an end to class and classes in the future. He saw that working people could only liberate themselves by liberating society as a whole; by dissolving classes altogether. There was nothing about class that made socialism inevitable, but the specific position and the experience of the working class under capitalism gave it an unrivalled insight into the way capitalism functions and the power to overcome it. It also gave it an interest in challenging every form of oppression in capitalist society.

This book goes on to look briefly at how subsequent history has been shaped by class struggles that have at times shaken capitalism's foundations. It outlines the extraordinary spread of socialist ideas and organisation in the years after Marx's death. Using amongst other things the World Labour Group Database developed by a group of US labour historians in the 1980s and 90s, it examines the extent and impact of the great cycles of working-class insurgency that followed.[12] It is hard for anyone to deny the importance of class in the years of turbulence and revolution that followed the First World War. Chapter three examines the significance of some of the highpoints of those years.

After that, however, the consensus is that class lost its radical edge. The period after the Second World War is normally presented as one dominated by social peace and the incorporation of the working class into a new social compact with capitalism. Chapter four challenges this idea. The post-war years of relative calm were the product of the defeat or containment of a wave of working-class insurgency and an unprecedented rise in the rate of profit. Class struggle didn't so much disappear as become depoliticised. The end of the boom reversed the terms of the equation. Alienation and apathy turned into a wave of anger that brought class back to the centre of the political stage. In reality, the period of the 'post-war consensus' was bookended by two of the three great peaks of twentieth-century class struggle, both of which presented real threats to the established order and raised the question of different ways of organising society.

In the process of re-examining some of the recent history of class struggle, the book puts the case that the ideas that Marx and subsequent revolutionaries have developed about class consciousness provide essential ways to understand the predicament we are in and plot a way out of it. Despite travesties and caricatures, the revolutionary tradition of Marxism has always attempted to understand the way class under capitalism can generate *both* resistance and passivity.

The great period of working-class insurgency after the First World War was accompanied by theoretical developments in the working-class movement on many fronts, but in particular a series of vitally important investigations into the interplay between class, consciousness and working-class organisation. This book puts the case that, despite serial misinterpretations, this revolutionary Marxist tradition has dealt more effectively than any other with the question of how an anti-capitalist consciousness periodically develops, but also how capitalism has managed to survive, despite the miseries it creates. It therefore provides an invaluable basis for discussions about the questions of strategy and organisation that face the left today.

Pessimism of the intellectuals

The setbacks for working-class struggle and organisation and the general retreat from class has had a damaging impact on the left. Opposition to neoliberalism has been weaker and more fragmented than it might have been, and has struggled to match the level of anger that has been generated. Social democracy's move away from class-based politics has disappointed, demoralised and disorientated working people. Matters were made worse by the move away from class amongst 'Post-Marxist' intellectuals from the 1970s, often taking their cue from French philosopher Louis Althusser. Under rightward pressure, even self-identifying Marxists have tended to shy away from an analysis that puts class at its centre. The tendency in radical thought to downplay class and class struggle has encouraged a retreat from a concrete analysis of the economic system and sometimes even any real consideration of how society as a whole functions. A focus on the experience of particular oppressed groups has enriched the movement, but sometimes defaulted to a politics of identity that fails to link particular oppressions to a wider understanding of society.

One result of the retreat from class on the left is that various forces on the right have been able to move in and construct 'ethnicised' working-class identities like 'the white working class' or to draw sections of working people into populist cross-class alliances with fake anti-elite credentials. These projects are of course toxic. In reality, they tie workers to particular fractions of the ruling group, reinforce divisions and deflect popular anger against vulnerable groups in terrible ways. The spread of such right-wing identitarian politics in all its forms is one more pressing argument for the revival of an authentic politics of class that can start pointing to real solutions for the mass of the population.

For all the challenges that the left faces, pessimistic assessments tend to ignore the fact that there is a clarifying side to the popular experience of capitalism and the struggle against it. There is still a low level of industrial action in most parts of the world, but this should not be mistaken for complete passivity or co-option amongst workers. Neoliberalism has generated widespread discontent. The resulting radicalisation has produced a record level of social mobilisation.[13] Millions have participated in enormous social movements, from the great anti-capitalist protests at the turn of the century to the anti-war movement that followed it, a variety of rebellions against austerity after the 2008 banking crisis, a series of mass democracy movements and waves of popular opposition to climate change and institutional racism. Working people were always involved and were often central to these movements.

Class is in fact starting to make a comeback. As neoliberal capitalism has proved incapable of solving society's increasingly pressing problems, even of restoring profitability, attention has begun to turn towards the almost unimaginable divisions it has created, and the damage done. Poll after poll is showing increased opposition to inequality and the overweening power of big business. To the surprise of the pessimists and despite the weakness of the left, huge numbers of people have started to identify with socialism.[14] Meanwhile, after years of fragmentation, tendencies towards the concentration of capital have created new centres of potential working-class strength and new vulnerabilities for the employers.

The Covid pandemic has served to re-focus attention on the crucial role played by workers with some of the lowest pay and lowest status in society, appropriately renamed 'key workers'. In many countries, a labour shortage whose origins predated the pandemic has also exposed the indispensability of working-class people and at the same time provided extra leverage.

Unions in some places are growing, new organising initiatives are being tried and there are signs of renewed confidence amongst workers to fight.[15]

As the accounts that follow show, class struggle doesn't tend to rise on a gradual incline. Rather it escalates suddenly and explosively in leaps and waves. Since the second half of the nineteenth century, there has been a succession of such massive outbreaks of unrest. Insurgent struggles in the years before and after the First World War, following the Second World War, and from the mid-1960s to the late 1970s affected all the core capitalist countries and reverberated way beyond them. As a whole range of studies have shown, they were the result of accumulated tensions which ignited suddenly after years of compression. They arose at the intersection of dramatic economic and technological change with wider social crisis, often including war, and the failure of the established politics to deal with the needs and aspirations of new, radicalised working populations.[16]

Making detailed predictions of how such complex processes are likely to play out in the future would be foolhardy. It would however be equally mistaken for the left to ignore the fact that many of the characteristics that marked these great upsurges can be observed around us. It is not just that the working class continues to exist, but that working people are angry, alienated and much more active than is usually recognised, all in the context of a multi-level crisis in society. The argument here is that it is to this set of challenges that the left must turn if it is to make progress.

2. A Universal Class

The current denial of class is only an extreme case of a long-held aversion. Ever since independent working-class organisation emerged in the 1830s and 1840s, discussing class has been regarded as improper in polite society. The writing of history, which had from time to time recognised class and even class struggles as central to human development, defaulted to the celebration of evolution and progress or the mere description of facts and events. Classical economics, which up to then had admitted certain contradictions in capitalism, morphed in the mid-nineteenth century into the purely mathematical harmonies of vulgar liberalism. In philosophy, Hegel's dialectics fell out of favour and were replaced either by mechanical materialism, various forms of idealism or, as in Nietzsche, an extreme subjectivity which openly declared, 'The true world is unattainable, it cannot be proved, it cannot promise anything.'[17] Sociology emerged in the second half of the nineteenth century as a science of society which recognised various connections between the individual and society but went out of its way to avoid making class central to its analysis.[18]

The establishment's attempt to bury the whole notion of class should not be at all surprising. Denying or suppressing class is in fact an ideological necessity for our rulers. To maintain legitimacy, the capitalist class and its supporters need to do everything possible to distract attention from the fact of their minority rule, the economics on which it is based and the conflicts of interests it generates. In the words of Hungarian Marxist Georg Lukács:

> ...the rule of the bourgeoisie can only be the rule of the minority. Its hegemony is exercised not merely *by* a minority but *in the interest* of that minority, so the need to deceive

the other classes and to ensure their class consciousness remains amorphous is inescapable for a bourgeois regime. (Consider here the theory of the state that stands 'above' class antagonisms, or the notion of an impartial system of justice).[19]

Suppressing the reality of class is also important for the confidence of the capitalists themselves. Their fighting spirit partly depends on the belief in the universality of their mission, so it is natural that their ideological history involves denying every insight into the divided, class nature of the society they have created. Every attempt is made to present the characteristics of capitalist society as natural and eternal rather than social and historical. Greed, competition and the urge to own private property are all explained as expressions of a timeless human nature. Various forms of oppression are justified by the inherent characteristics of those being oppressed. The abstract individual is celebrated as the irreducible element in society. As we shall see, this ideological job is made easier by the way capitalism tends to obscure real social relations by turning everything into commodities. As a result, underlying capitalist relations can take on the appearance of free exchange between disconnected, equal agents.

The argument of this book is that the great moments of radicalism and hope for change over the last two hundred years have all been times when class has reasserted itself in the face of this denial. The historical sketches that follow will show that sustained class struggle has a unique ability to destabilise the status quo. They also show that, almost by their nature, great class struggles create turmoil which tends to raise fundamental questions about existing society and how things should be run. The interaction between these two things, the social ferment and the intellectual radicalisation generated by class struggle, is the book's central concern. To begin to understand it we must start with the great investigation of class and class struggle that Marx and his closest comrade Engels carried out as the working-class movement first emerged.

Marx's breakthrough

Marx didn't discover class. As he pointed out, bourgeois historians and economists had regularly used the concept before him.[20] By the early 1830s, ten years before Marx started writing, radicals in Britain were beginning to organise a consciously working-class movement for the first time. In 1833, Irish-born radical Bronterre O'Brien, who went on to become a leader of the English Chartists, wrote as follows:

> An entire change in society – a change amounting to a complete subversion of the existing 'order of the world' – is contemplated by the working classes. They aspire to be at the top instead of at the bottom of society – or rather that there should be no bottom or top at all.[21]

Marx and Engels were, however, the first to fully grasp the explosive significance of class for understanding society and for changing it. Their work is often presented as being centred on blind, inevitable, economic processes. In fact, the opposite is true. Marx and Engels' ideas always had working-class self-activity at their heart because they saw in the working class the potential to overthrow economic necessity.

From 1840, Marx had read about the great workers' struggles led by the Chartists in Britain and he was kept up to date by Engels after they met in 1842. In October 1843 Karl Marx and his wife Jenny moved to Paris where they came into contact with advanced working-class activists in French socialist circles. In 1844 Marx wrote excitedly of the Silesian weavers' strike, the first major workers' struggle in his native Germany. Two insights had drawn him in this direction. The first, clear in his 1844 work *The Philosophical and Economic Notebooks*, was the intuition that the exploitation of workers was the key to understanding the general misery and disfunction of emerging capitalist society. Exploitation and the lack of control that workers had over their work and the economy generally – their 'alienation' – was the secret to the inhuman and barbaric nature of contemporary society as a whole.

Secondly, as a result, Marx and Engels argued that the working class was the key to the fight for human liberation. Up until then most left-wing radicals hadn't got beyond criticising the modern world, dreaming up utopian alternatives to it, demanding greater rights within it or plotting in secret societies to overthrow it. It was one thing to be a critic of capitalism and to seek liberation from it, but Marx recognised that theory had to become a material force. He saw in the working class a powerful group that had an interest in challenging the system. The working class was a real-world embodiment of practical and intellectual opposition to the system, it was 'poverty conscious of its spiritual and physical poverty, dehumanisation conscious of its own dehumanisation'.[22]

If the class nature of society pointed to how capitalism could be understood, challenged and potentially overthrown, then it followed that the way capitalism structured class had to be analysed in full. As a result, Marx and Engels focussed on how society works economically. *The German Ideology*, written by Marx and Engels in 1845 and 1846, was the first full account of their new approach. Its starting point was that to understand society you can't begin with the ideas it promotes, its morals or what people think about it. You have to grasp the way it is organised, its basic processes:

we do not set out from what men say, imagine, conceive, nor from men as narrated, thought of, imagined, conceived, in order to arrive at men in the flesh. We set out from real, active men, and on the basis of their real life-process we demonstrate the development of the ideological reflexes and echoes of this life-process. [23]

The 'real life process' was at root the way people produce. As people develop their productive forces, they develop certain relations with one another and with nature. These relations take on a life of their own. As Marx put it a year later, 'in the social production of their life, men enter into definite relations that are indispensable and independent of their will'. These relations constitute 'the economic structure of society'.[24]

For Marx, then, class was never just a label for people or a way of describing social hierarchies or exposing inequality, however important it is to highlight these things. Class had to be understood as an *active relation* between groups of people in society. It captures how people in their real lives are tied together in the economy. What was crucial for Marx was to grasp the 'active connection', the 'internal relation' between capital and labour, and to understand that it creates a deep contradiction at the heart of society, a living contradiction that alone opens the possibility of the overthrow of capitalist relations.[25]

In February 1848, the month Marx opened *The Communist Manifesto* with the line 'all history is the history of class struggle', revolution broke out across Europe. The revolutionaries were fighting for political democracy and their leaderships were middle class. In France, though, for the first time in history, working-class people set up their own barricades and moved into struggle for their own social demands in the face of the emerging capitalist class.

As a result, 1848 proved to be a turning point. The emergence of the working class as an independent force shook society. It scared the bourgeoisie to such an extent that they became forever fearful of revolution. It was at this point that the discussion of class fell completely out of fashion in bourgeois circles. Liberal economists dropped the notion of exploitation and abandoned any idea that labour was the source of value. Historians like Guizot, who had explained the French revolution of 1789 in terms of 'the various strata existing in society and their mutual relationships', gave up on class and turned to presenting history as a narrative, a sequence of events without inner logic.[26] Ever since, mainstream academics, politicians and journalists have tended to deny the existence of class, or if that wasn't possible, to break it down into multiple categories, treat it as one division amongst many or as purely a matter of culture.

Class under capitalism

Various class societies have existed since humans produced enough for a surplus; goods over and above what is needed to survive on a daily basis. But in capitalism class relations have reached their fullest development. Industrial capitalism has only been around for about two hundred years and when Marx started writing it only existed in the north-western corners of Europe and on parts of the eastern seaboard of the US. Since that time, it has transformed the globe. Industry has reached every part of the inhabited world, sucking billions of people from traditional, rural communities into giant cities and factories. In the length of time that it took previous societies to move from the hoe to the plough, capitalism has taken us from the hand mill to artificial intelligence via the steam engine, electricity, the internal combustion engine and space travel.

Exploitation in previous class societies was driven by the immediate needs of the rulers. In the Middle Ages feudal lords used the surplus they extracted from the peasants to fund their armies and their own relatively luxurious lifestyles. Max Weber paraphrased Marx's view of the feudal economy well when he said 'the limits to the exploitation of the feudal serf were determined by the walls of the stomach of the feudal lord'.[27] The unique characteristic of capitalism is that the expansion of wealth has become an end in itself: capitalism is driven by competition without limit to accumulate capital. In order to survive, the capitalists have to try constantly to increase their profits so that they can generate new investment. This they need to do to achieve the economies of scale and buy the new technology necessary to keep prices competitive and stay in business. This is what explains its dynamism, the speed with which capitalism came to dominate the globe and the ruthlessness with which it exploits workers.

It has led to a situation in which, more than any previous society, a singular economic relation, that between capital and labour, dominates. As Marx wrote in the *Grundrisse*, there is in all class societies, 'one specific kind of production which predominates over the rest, whose relations thus assign rank and influence to the others. It is a general illumination which bathes all the other colours and modifies their particularity. It is a particular ether which determines the specific gravity of every being which has materialized within it.'[28] But in developed capitalism, commodity production shapes society to an unprecedented degree. It has above all simplified class relations:

> In the earlier epochs of history, we find almost everywhere a complicated arrangement of society into various orders, a manifold gradation of social rank. In ancient Rome we have patricians, knights, plebeians, slaves; in the Middle Ages, feudal lords, vassals, guild-masters, journeymen, apprentices, serfs; in almost all of these classes, again, subordinate gradations.
>
> The modern bourgeois society that has sprouted from the ruins of feudal society has not done away with class antagonisms. It has but established new classes, new conditions of oppression, new forms of struggle in place of the old ones.
>
> Our epoch, the epoch of the bourgeoisie, possesses,

however, this distinct feature: it has simplified class antagonisms. Society as a whole is more and more splitting up into two great hostile camps, into two great classes directly facing each other — Bourgeoisie and Proletariat.[29]

Marx's method was characterised by first identifying the *essential trends* and then elaborating how they and other elements combine in 'a rich totality of many determinations and relationships'.[30] The relationship between the bourgeoisie, the owners of capital, and the workers, whose labour expanded capital, was the determining relationship in society. This doesn't of course mean that other classes didn't exist. Marx spends a great deal of time describing intermediate classes, discussing for example the nature of the peasantry and the role of various professionals.

In a fascinating series of discussions of the role of intellectuals, for instance, Marx points out that the noun 'intellectual' was a *creation* of emerging capitalism. For Marx, the emergence of a new stratum of intellectuals was a result of two things. The first was that capitalists tend to be more actively involved in their work than were the previous land-owning ruling classes and were therefore too preoccupied with making profit to make much philosophy. For this reason, they needed to develop a separate group from outside their ranks to 'cultivate the class's illusion about itself'.[31] This tendency was reinforced by the deskilling of labour and the resulting separation of work and technical knowledge accompanying the development of capitalism. Together, these trends led to a divorce between thinking and doing.

In general, Marx understood that professional intellectuals, dependent as they tended to be on the dominant class, were 'drawn to the same problems and solutions' as their masters and tended to 'give a suitable high-flown expression to the universal fantasy spinning and indifference'.[32] At the same time, as capitalism developed, there was a growing need for mental labour as part of the process of production. Engineers and clerks were necessary as well as overlookers and managers. Intellectual and manual labour were separating, but they were all part of the production process in different ways and the commodity produced was 'the common product of these persons'.[33]

Class position depended on people's relationship to the process of production. Intellectuals and managers were part of a middle class that in different ways imposed the interests of the ruling class. There were other forms of mental labour that were being routinised and incorporated directly into 'the living production machine', creating what Marx called 'the collective labourer', the connected combination of different working people.[34]

Losing control

Work under capitalism is called 'free labour', but for the vast majority, this is a negative freedom which actually ensures the complete domination of capital over working lives. In feudal society, peasants had a formal relationship of subservience to their lords. They worked their own land and had access to the commons as long as they gave up a proportion of their product or their labour to the lord. In return, the lord was expected to protect them. The emerging capitalist class challenged these arrangements.

The fixed non-commercial relations between the peasant and the lord held back the development of production for the market. The capitalists wanted the land to cultivate commercially, and they needed to free people from the land to work in the new industries developing in the towns. All traditional arrangements not based on the market economy were a block to expanding capitalist production. Despite the myth of a spontaneously emerging free market, in reality the bourgeoisie fought long and hard to impose its model on society. They challenged the feudal establishment for power, brutally cleared and seized common land, abolished the old mechanisms for looking after the poor and took control of state apparatuses. The result was that for the first time the mass of labourers lost control over both the means of production and their products.

Capitalism then is a system in which working people are completely dependent on capital for their livelihoods; for their very existence. The vast majority have nowhere else to go in order to make a living. Supporters of capitalism may claim it is based on free choice. It is true that workers may in some circumstances be able to choose between different employers, but those employers will all be competing to maximise profits, meaning they will all be trying to drive wages down to the minimum and constantly pressurising staff to work faster and more efficiently. As a result, capitalism has the reproduction of inequality built into its basic economic drives.

Labour is the source of all profits. It is only human labour that can add value in the production process. But, in capitalist society, this ability to transform the world is turned against the worker: 'It is true that labour produces marvels for the rich, but it produces privation for the worker.' It leads not just to misery at work but a deep sense of estrangement or alienation of the essential human capacity of labour:

> ...the more the worker exerts himself in his work, the more powerful becomes the alien world of objects which he creates over and against himself, the poorer he and his inner world become, and the less they belong to him...in his work, therefore, he does not affirm himself but denies himself, does not feel content but unhappy, does not develop freely his physical and mental energy but mortifies his body and ruins his mind. The worker therefore only feels himself outside his work, and in his work feels outside himself. He feels at home when he is not working, and when he is working he does not feel at home.[35]

The competition between capitals creates a permanent drive to increase workers' productivity. The cheaper a capitalist can produce per unit, the greater will be their market share and therefore their slice of the profits in the system overall. This creates virtually constant upheaval in workers' lives.

There are a number of ways for capitalists to try to increase productivity. One is to lengthen hours or lower pay by attacking the conditions of existing workers, cutting staff numbers or sacking the entire workforce and moving the enterprise to a lower-wage zone. Another is to introduce labour-saving technology, so that the number of goods produced per wage are increased. In both cases, workers tend to suffer. Where in previous societies people may have expected to make more when they work harder, in the absence of workers' resistance, capitalism forces them to work harder for the same pay.

In conditions of commodity production, labour-saving technology that could benefit society as a whole actually increases workers' alienation by de-skilling, intensifying the division of labour and increasing management's control over every aspect of the work experience:

> Factory work exhausts the nervous system to the uttermost, it does away with the many-sided play of the muscles, and confiscates every atom of freedom, both in bodily and intellectual activity...The special skill of each individual insignificant factory operative vanishes as an infinitesimal quantity before the science, the gigantic physical forces, and mass of labour that are embodied in the factory mechanism and, together, with that mechanism, constitute the power of the master.[36]

The result is that human beings at work are turned into something approaching the machines we serve. The familiar experience of clock watching at work, the desperate wait for the end of the shift, is not just an indicator of boredom, it is evidence that at work our humanity is suspended, that we have been reduced to hyper-regulated instruments for capital's self-expansion. 'Time is everything, man is nothing; he is, at the most, time's carcase.'[37]

Working lives under capitalism are then in reality unfree, but the prison world of capitalism doesn't end at the gates of the warehouse or the factory or the office. The nature of the capital/labour relationship affects all social relations; every aspect of society. In every country, as it won power, the capitalist class reshaped ruling institutions, set up new education systems and civil services and introduced police forces and new systems of justice.

All these are moulded to ensure the dominance of the capitalist class and promote their interests. Levels of welfare are set to keep people just above destitution. Working-class education tends to emphasise discipline and uncritical learning by rote. The police are trained to be particularly hostile to workers when they organise. From the courts to the parliament, these institutions of power are shrouded in elite ceremony and mystification. All this disciplines workers, keeps them out of positions of influence and attempts to reproduce a state of deference, insecurity and even fear. It amounts to a mechanics of oppression that supports and reinforces the exploitation that takes place in work.

These institutions, however, are also riven by class. The state must ensure the continuing functioning of society generally as well as maintain the status quo. This involves the creation of a layer of functionaries who aren't necessarily productive in the sense of generating commodities or profit, but whose work is essential for the continued production of profit more generally. Their wages or salaries are paid out of the proceeds of capital accumulation in the form of taxes. Their labour forms an integral part of capitalist production which is 'not merely the production of commodities, it is essentially the production of surplus-value'.[38] Given that state bodies are largely funded out of profits, managements are needed to try and enforce 'efficiency' very much along the lines of directly productive sectors. The actual producers of state services, where they are not involved in the direct repression of workers, as in the police and military, are as much part of the working class as are those that directly produce profits.

Counter-power

It is not surprising that Marx's concept of class is unpopular in the mainstream. Marx's picture of a brutally divided society with organised robbery at its heart amounts to a devastating moral condemnation of capitalism. It also directly contradicts the various ways in which the establishment want us to understand the world we live in. Their preferred model of society is a giant market in which individuals interact freely and equally. In reality, of course, individuals are born into society with drastically different levels of wealth. Marx stressed however that it is the way *production* is organised that more than anything shapes society. 'The arrangement of distribution,' he says in *Capital*, 'is entirely dependent on the arrangement of production.'[39] What people consume, even what people regard as needs, depends in the first instance on what is produced in any given society. The way the goods are distributed depends on the distribution of wealth, itself determined by one's position in the productive process.[40]

Politicians also like to tell us 'We are all in it together.' This illusion can only gain traction because the economy appears to operate independently of human will and control. The idea can't survive contact with an understanding that the whole system is driven by a tiny minority forcing profit from the labour of the many. We are also told that capitalist investors are 'wealth creators'. Looked at from the point of view of class, the capital that an investor brings to the table has been extracted – stolen –

from past labour. The investor is simply recycling the spoils to make still more money.

Marxism also challenges the idea that capitalism will 'lift up' the poor over time. Capitalism has produced unimaginable wealth, but as Marx predicted, its drive to keep wages down means that for most of its existence the distribution of that wealth has become more and more unequal. Forty years of neoliberal capitalism has brought us to the extraordinary point at which just eight men are worth as much as half the world's population.[41] Marx's analysis leads to the devastating conclusion that the poor are poor *because* the rich are rich. Generalised poverty and inequality are a necessary outcome of a system based on competition for profit.

The most radical aspect of all of Marx's class analysis is however that it shows that in the process of conquering the world and achieving by far the highest levels of exploitation in history, capitalism has created its own nemesis, its own 'grave digger' in the working class. Marx believed workers had the potential to overthrow existing conditions for a number of reasons. The first was directly economic. The fact that workers are denied the material benefits of a more and more productive society gave them an immediate interest in resistance. The second was that the degradation experienced by most of humanity under capitalism was concentrated in the working class. The denial of human self-fulfilment, the 'notorious crime of the whole of society', was most acutely experienced in exploitation and its attendant alienation. Workers have through their experience the most acute consciousness of the immensely destructive and degrading capacities of capitalist accumulation.

Secondly, as well as having an interest in change, workers have the means to make it happen. Just as workers rely entirely on capitalists for their livelihood, capitalists are completely dependent on workers for their profits. Powerless as individuals, collectively, workers have immense potential power. As Marx put it, 'of all the instruments of production, the greatest productive power is the revolutionary class itself'.[42] By forcing huge numbers of workers together at the point of production, capitalism creates a counter-power. Struggles over pay and conditions have the capacity to generalise into a political conflict between different class organisations:

> Large-scale industry concentrates in one place a crowd of people unknown to one another. Competition divides their interests. But the maintenance of wages, this common interest which they have against their boss, unites them in a common thought of resistance – *combination*...If the first aim of resistance was merely the maintenance of wages, combinations, at first isolated, constitute themselves into groups as the capitalists in their turn unite for the purpose of repression, and in the face of always united capital, the maintenance of the association becomes more necessary to them than that of wages...In this struggle – a veritable civil war – all the elements necessary for a coming battle unite and develop. Once it has reached this point, association takes on a political character.[43]

The exclusion of workers from the fruits of production and from any stake in society leads to a final, crucial characteristic. Capitalism has created a class which has no interest in exploiting or oppressing any other group. All previous revolutions, including the bourgeois revolution, resulted in the replacement of one ruling class by another. The emerging capitalist class fought against the localism, the fixed bonds and the backwardness of the feudal system, but they did so to establish a new more dynamic regime of exploitation. Because the economic project of the bourgeoisie depended on the exploitation of a new class, the new rights it offered for the great mass of people, even at their most radical, were limited to the realm of politics. The French Revolution that began in 1789 was the quintessential bourgeois revolution. For all its achievements, the equality announced in its central slogan of 'liberty, fraternity and equality' turned out to be at best formal and political rather than material or economic.

The nature of the subordination and exploitation of workers puts them in a much more radical situation. Not only is the working class unable to exploit any other group, but for working people, political freedom without social and economic liberation counts for little. Real liberation for workers can only come by dismantling the whole edifice of society. For the working class, the end of its exploitation and oppression can only mean the end of the whole system, the end of all oppression, and the end of class itself. As Marx wrote in *The Communist Manifesto*:

> All previous historical movements were movements of minorities, or in the interest of minorities. The proletarian movement is the self-conscious, independent movement of the immense majority, in the interest of the immense majority. The proletariat, the lowest stratum of our present society, cannot stir, cannot raise itself up, without the whole superincumbent strata of official society being sprung into the air.[44]

This was the central insight of Marxism, one to which Marx returned again and again. Workers 'formed a class which cannot emancipate itself without...emancipating all other spheres of society' he wrote in 1844.[45] The next year, he and Engels wrote that the proletariat cannot liberate itself 'without destroying the conditions of its own life...without destroying all the inhuman conditions in life in contemporary society which exist in the proletariat in concentrated form'.[46] The sheer comprehensiveness of its exploitation and oppression made the working class a subversive force like no other, 'a class which is the dissolution of all classes', a class in short, 'with radical chains'.[47]

The structures of oppression

Grasping that it is in the interests of workers to oppose oppression is very different from reducing oppression to the question of class. Both Marx and Engels were in fact very concerned with the *specific mechanisms* that led to particular oppressions. In the *German Ideology*, for example, they traced the origins of women's oppression to changing family relations which, while related to wider historical developments, have their own dynamic:

> Thus when monogamous marriage first makes its appearance in history, it is not as the reconciliation of man and woman, still less as the highest form of such a reconciliation. Quite the contrary. Monogamous marriage comes on the scene as the subjugation of the one sex by the other; it announces a struggle between the sexes unknown throughout the whole previous prehistoric period.[48]

Engels developed this analysis in *The Origins of the Family, Private Property and the State,* where he argued the development of the family was linked to the rise of private property. The association of property with the family household led to the idea that it should be heritable through the family. This in turn led to what Engels called 'the historic defeat of the female sex' because in order to ensure that their property could be inherited by their biological children, men sought to control the women with whom they wanted to have children. This was the source of the patriarchal family, the key organising structure of women's oppression.

Marx returned to the issue of women's oppression and the changing role of the family repeatedly in his writings, in fact he saw the extent to which women were free and equal as an index of the progress of society. A number of things stand out from these reflections. One is that he stressed the importance of recognising that women's oppression affected all women in society, albeit in different ways. In an essay on suicide, Marx describes how sexual and physical abuse and repressive family relations led three bourgeois women to take their lives. He points as a result to the need for a total transformation of the family.[49]

The second is that his discussions of the relations between work and family life are dialectical and nuanced, not at all reductionist as is sometimes claimed. In *Capital*, for example, Marx wrote that as women entered the workforce, they potentially gained power in their private lives since they now contributed financially to the family's upkeep and they were no longer under the control of a man at home all day. On the other hand, long working hours for women and men tended to undermine the family and lead to a situation in which children were not properly cared for. In a later passage he draws the conclusion that these developments too point in the direction of 'a higher form of family' in which women and men could be true equals.[50]

Marx and Engels approached racism too as a product of complex historical developments with their own dynamics that needed to be carefully studied and challenged. Marx identified anti-Irish racism for example as one product of the brutal colonisation of Ireland by the English:

> The ordinary English worker hated the Irish worker as a competitor who lowers his standard of life. In relation to the Irish worker he feels himself a member of the *ruling* nation and so turns himself *against Ireland,* thus strengthening their domination *over himself.*[51]

Marx saw a parallel situation in the US where the racism generated to justify slavery poisoned the minds of the white population. 'Every independent movement of the workers,' he wrote, 'was paralysed so long as slavery disfigured a part of the Republic. Labour with a white skin cannot emancipate itself where labour with a black skin is branded.'[52] Once these patterns had been established, they were deliberately sustained by the ruling class to keep working people divided. The British establishment, for example, worked hard to fan the flames of anti-Irish racism, which was 'artificially kept alive and intensified by the press, the pulpit, the comic papers, in short, by all the means at the disposal of the ruling classes'. For Marx, such racism was 'the secret of the *impotence of the English working class'*.[53]

Given the extent to which mechanisms of oppression were embedded in the structures of society, combatting oppression required much more than simple appeals for unity. Specific and concerted struggle was needed. Marx and Engels were particularly proud of the record of British workers in supporting the struggle of the northern US states against the slave-owning south in the US Civil War. They themselves were centrally involved in organising a campaign against the oppression of the Irish in England. Under Marx's leadership, the General Council of the International made supporting the Irish a central plank of their agitation in Britain.

In 1872, council members backed a massive demonstration to Hyde Park demanding freedom for 42 Irish prisoners held by the Gladstone government. The government banned the march, but organisers went ahead anyway. Engels was elated. He reported on the demonstration for an Italian radical paper:

This is the first time an Irish demonstration has been held in Hyde Park; it was very successful and even the London bourgeois press cannot deny this. It is also the first time the English and Irish sections of our population have united in friendship. These two elements of the working class, whose enmity towards each other was so much in the interests of the government and wealthy classes, are now offering one another the hand of friendship; this gratifying fact is due principally to the influence of the last General Council of the International, which has always directed all its efforts to unite the workers of both peoples on a basis of complete equality. This meeting, of the 3rd November, will usher in a new era in the history of London's working-class movement.[54]

There are a number of conclusions from all this, which together have an important bearing on contemporary discussions about oppression. Firstly, adopting the idea that oppressions are embedded in the economy of society in particular ways is not to downplay their importance. It is in fact the very opposite. It involves facing up to the *seriousness* of the issues by recognising that oppressions are deep seated and tenacious because they are a product of the central drives of the system. It is to argue that fighting oppression is not just a matter of recognising particular identities, of persuasion or changing peoples' attitudes, or even of winning political rights, important though those things are. It has to involve challenging the power structure itself.

Seeing oppressions in this way as structured around the needs of capital leads to a second conclusion. If we reject the idea of class as an identity, and understand it, like Marx, as the driving *social relation* in society, class becomes absolutely central to the project of wider human liberation. Because of their economic position, organised working people have a unique power and capacity to paralyse the system and to begin to supersede it. In Marx's view such a transformation was necessary to liberate the whole of society. That liberation remains, however, only *a possibility*. The insight that the working-class movement has an interest in opposing all oppression doesn't mean class struggle will automatically overcome oppression by itself. What is needed is for the movement to understand, consciously expose and combat every aspect of oppression in order to root it out effectively.

There is a two-way movement here. Marx and Engels fought for political freedoms, for equal rights, against discrimination, for universal suffrage, for all the promises offered and rarely delivered by the bourgeois revolutions. These struggles were important in themselves, and they were crucial in overcoming divisions amongst working people. Marx and Engels also understood however that oppression could not finally be overcome by purely political means. The separation of the political from the economic is one of capitalism's survival strategies. Restricting struggles to political rights means leaving untouched the structures and forces that generate oppression in the first place. A fight to the finish against oppression requires tackling every instance of discrimination and injustice directly. It also means however taking on the economic system from which they flow and confronting the state that defends them.

In itself or for itself

The question of how radical ideas can emerge under capitalism is bound to be a central issue for all who want to see fundamental social change. For Marx and Engels, the development of class consciousness amongst workers was key. They contended that because of workers' location in the economy, because of their role as society's producers and because of their exploitation, workers were in a unique position from which to grasp the way the system works. Gaining these insights was, however, far from being an automatic process.

The previous discussion of oppression points to one of the great myths about Marx and Engels; that they were determinists, believing that socialism was an inevitable outcome of the dynamics of capitalism. The criticism is particularly ironic as it is often made by supporters of the free market who actually do believe that economic forces *should* determine human outcomes. Both Marx and Engels occasionally came up with formulations which can be taken out of context to support a certain fatalism, and many of Marx's followers fell into the trap of embracing it. In fact, however, the reason Marxism is so loathed by supporters of the status quo is precisely because it seeks a *way out* of economic coercion to collective freedom, an end to our present 'prehistory' to a real history made by humans through the establishment of conscious, democratic control over all aspects of society.

Marxism identifies existing material constraints on human activity, recognising that people make history 'not in conditions of their own choosing', and that as a result that to be viable, strategies for liberation have to be rooted in social reality. For Marx, though, the aim of socialism was precisely to expand personal freedom, to end the domination of external circumstances over our lives. Even in the here and now, he pointed out, even when we are not in control of our destinies, it is active human beings that produce and distribute goods, keep institutions running and society functioning. This active reality of human existence, not historical inevitability, is at the heart of Marxism. 'All social life is essentially practical,' Marx wrote in 1845 as he was formulating his new ideas, 'all mysteries which lead theory to mysticism find their rational solution in human practice and the comprehension of this practice.'[55]

Marx and Engels were focussed precisely on trying to make workers aware of the significance of their own actions. It is one thing to have the collective power to make change happen. It is another to be conscious of it. Marx made the distinction between workers' objective position in society as a 'class in itself' and a fully conscious class as a 'class for itself': a class which understood its own situation, its own role and the possibilities this opened up. The working class becoming conscious, becoming a class 'for itself', was the precondition for changing society.

As a result of this understanding, Marx and Engels were deeply involved in many of the key political struggles of their time and they were almost always part of some kind of militant organisation. In the 1840s they were involved in the League of the Just which developed into the Communist League. During the revolutions of 1848 they regarded themselves as being on the extreme left of the democratic revolution which they hoped would grow into workers' revolution. When the International Working Men's Association, or First International, was formed in 1864, Marx quickly became its most prominent figure. It was Marx's support for the Paris Commune in 1871 that brought him international fame and notoriety.

Marx and Engel's involvement in political activism is itself evidence that they understood the success of workers' struggle was far from inevitable. At the same time, this involvement provided them with insights into the problems and possibilities of that struggle. They never wrote down their ideas about class consciousness in one place, but scattered theoretical comments and reflections on their activism can be pieced together into an account of the key factors they believed were involved.

The central point here runs completely contrary to much of the received wisdom about Marxism, and it is a very important starting point for any serious discussion of radical politics and how to achieve change. This is that there were, in Marx's view, *two sides* to workers' experience and understanding under capitalism. There are aspects of working people's social existence that hold back radicalisation and there are others that are subversive, that promote resistance and politicisation. Grasping both sides of this experience, and how they interact, is essential to understanding how a critical consciousness can develop.

Perhaps the most common explanation for passivity or acceptance of the status quo is the influence of the media, the education system and ruling-class ideas generally. Marx discussed these things in the *German Ideology*:

The ideas of the ruling class are in every epoch the ruling

ideas, i.e. the class which is the ruling material force of society, is at the same time its ruling intellectual force. The class which has the means of material production at its disposal, has control at the same time over the means of mental production, so that thereby, generally speaking, the ideas of those who lack the means of mental production are subject to it.[56]

This is a constant factor with real importance, and the power of the media and the education system is the thing that most people think of first when they seek to explain the system's survival. On further investigation, however, it becomes clear that its explanatory power is limited. Looking simply to ruling-class ideas doesn't help us understand either the fact that workers almost always hold *some* radical and oppositional ideas in their heads, or that working-class consciousness varies over time.

Ever the materialist, Marx in fact concentrated on the nature of working-class *experience* under capitalism to explain the complexities of consciousness. There are elements of this experience that discourage resistance and obscure underlying realities. Workers as we have seen are 'alienated'; they lack control over the production process which appears to be operating completely independently of them. Marx argued that the fact that we produce a social world without controlling it affects the way we see it and understand it. Contradictions that are not resolved in reality can be falsely resolved in the mind's eye. In Marx's words, 'if in all ideology men and their circumstances appear upside-down as in a *camera obscura*, this phenomenon arises just as much from their historical life-process as the inversion of objects on the retina does from their physical life-process'.[57]

The drive to maximise profits leads to extreme and inhuman division of labour, to ruthless discipline, regulation and monitoring of every movement. The result is devastating.

The fragmentation of the process of the production leads to the fragmentation of the human. This experience encourages passivity, a sense of powerlessness and an inability to grasp the overall nature of the process of production in which workers are involved.

The result is that the actual processes humans are engaged in are diminished and the productions of social labour take on what appears to be an independent character. The commodities we collectively produce come to dominate our lives and even our thinking. Marx called this 'reification', or 'commodity fetishism', a phrase that was meant to indicate that, like a primitive fetish, the commodity appears to take on a life of its own even though it is human-made. All this has the effect of concealing the real relations of production. The structure of the wage system is the obvious case in point. The exchange that takes place between the worker and the capitalist is actually unequal. The capitalist pays the worker a good deal less than the value she or he produces. But because the capitalist only makes good on that value when the commodity reaches the market, and because the market appears to operate quite independently of human agency, the robbery is hidden. The contract between worker and employer appears fair to both sides because it too is determined by market rates. This reification affects every aspect of our life and takes its purest form in money, which Marx called 'the universal pimp'. In the marketplace we all appear to be equal:

> A worker who buys a loaf of bread and a millionaire who does the same appear in this act only as simple buyers, just as, in respect of them, the grocer appears only as a seller. All other aspects here are extinguished. The *content* of these purchases, like their *extent,* here appears irrelevant when compared with the formal aspect.[58]

Meanwhile, the relative autonomy and the chaotic tendencies

of the market mean that the legal system and the civil service have to maintain some independence from the rest of the ruling class in order to regulate relations between competing capitalist interests, and to adjudicate between them. This can give the state, fundamentally rooted in the interests of the ruling class, the appearance of being above the fray. Taken together, all these factors can have a profoundly mystifying effect on people's understanding of the world.

There are then important aspects of capitalist reality that obscure the robbery at the system's heart, that atomise workers and hinder the development of a clear class consciousness. These aspects of life are the soil in which the individualistic ideas of the ruling class can take root. This interaction between ruling-class ideas and the alienated experience of life under capitalism is, however, only one side of the story. There are other decisive aspects to working-class experience. First of all, the inequality in society and the compulsion at the heart of the labour process is never completely hidden. The flip side of workers' lack of control over the labour process is the despotism of the management. Workers are:

> Slaves of the bourgeois class, and of the bourgeois state; they are daily and hourly enslaved by the machine, by the overlooker, and, above all, by the individual bourgeois manufacturer himself. The more openly this despotism proclaims gain to be its end and aim, the more hateful and embittering it is.[59]

Operating in these conditions tends to make people want to defend themselves and at least mitigate the worst excesses of exploitation. That is why trade-union organisation has sprung up almost everywhere, why there are social-democratic or reformist parties in so many countries and why so many workers have voted for them. It is why there is always some level of working-class consciousness and some level of resistance. But though life under capitalism often forces people to organise to improve their conditions and vote for parties that promise reforms, it doesn't immediately lead to *revolutionary* consciousness. Even when they resist, people tend to start out with a sectional understanding of their work process. The division of labour obscures the way the different elements of the economy fit together and the associated alienation makes people feel atomised.

How can these limitations be overcome? How can workers break through the partial delusions generated by capitalist reality itself? Once again, Marx's solution is eminently materialist. Workers' consciousness, he argued, changes most radically when workers start to fight back themselves. The imperatives of active struggle against management often force people to overcome sectionalism and look for solidarity from workers in other departments or industries. Major struggles further radicalise people when the police, the media or the government get involved. Workers in these circumstances start to see who their real allies and who their enemies are, and begin to put together a picture of their real position in society. Most of all, active resistance tends to breed confidence in workers' own capacities and their importance in society.

The breakthrough that led to the first complete outline of the Marxist worldview involved recognising precisely this; the significance of working-class struggle. It is for this reason above all that the idea that Marxism is fatalistic or deterministic is so mistaken. Our first sight of this breakthrough comes in Marx's hastily scribbled notes which were later called the *Theses on Feuerbach*. Engels called this 'the first document in which is deposited the brilliant germ of the new world outlook'.[60] Marx wrote the notes in 1845 as preparation for the *German Ideology*. The *Theses* marked the definitive break from the fatalism of the kind of materialism that dominated up to that point. In the

Theses, Marx argued it is not enough to understand that people are shaped by their circumstances, you have to recognise that those circumstances themselves are created by human beings. They are created first by human labour, but also by another kind of transformative practice, the struggle for social change. When people start to collectively try and change the world around them, they start to change themselves.

In the third of the theses, Marx identified this coming together of changing of circumstances and self-change as 'revolutionary practice'. The way was now clear for Marx and Engels to write the rousing and crucial final paragraph of part of the *German Ideology*. Here, they argued that revolutionary or communist consciousness is the product more than anything of mass movements for change:

> Both for the production on a mass scale of this communist consciousness, and for the success of the cause itself, the alteration of men on a mass scale is necessary, an alteration which can only take place in a practical movement, a revolution; this revolution is necessary, therefore, not only because the ruling class cannot be overthrown in any other way, but also because the class overthrowing it can only in a revolution succeed in ridding itself of all the muck of ages and become fitted to found society anew.[61]

Fortune and force

What factors determined whether struggle would reach this level? What were the circumstances in which resistance might generalise to the point of becoming anti-systemic? For Marx and Engels, both the economic fortunes of capitalism at any particular time and the outcome of previous class struggles were crucial. The years after the defeat of the 1848 revolutions, for example, were marked by passivity and demoralisation on the part of the working class across Europe. Marx and Engels observed that the impact of the defeat, combined with the expansion of capitalism and colonialism from the 1850s on, meant British workers' leaders tended to adopt nationalist ideas and look towards middle-class parliamentary leadership:

> While the rout of their continental brethren unmanned the English working classes, and broke their faith in their own cause, it restored to the landlord and the money lord their somewhat shaken confidence. They insolently withdrew concessions already advertised. The discoveries of new gold lands led to an immense exodus, leaving an irreparable void in the ranks of the British proletariat. Others of its formerly active members were caught by the temporary bribe of greater work and wages...and in point of fact never before seemed the English working class so thoroughly reconciled to a state of political nullity.[62]

The kind of politics and organisation that workers adopted was crucial too. Marx and Engels never believed that the spontaneous struggle of workers would be enough on its own to overcome unevenness, sectionalism or illusions. No struggle takes place in a political vacuum, it always involves the conscious or unconscious adoption of particular strategies, which always crystallises out into different politics and forms of organisation.

Marx and Engels would never have been so polemical and so fixated on organisation if they hadn't believed that ideas and organisation were of decisive importance. They were amongst the first socialists to see the importance of trade-union struggle. Many on the left at the time thought that struggling for better wages was pointless, as market rates would re-impose themselves whatever the outcome of particular struggles. With his constant stress on the importance of self-activity, Marx disagreed, calling strikes 'the indispensable means of holding up the spirit of the labouring classes, of combining them into one great association against the encroachments of the ruling class, and of preventing them from becoming apathetic'. Engels agreed:

> The active resistance of the English working men has its effect in holding the money-greed of the bourgeoisie within certain limits, and keeping alive the opposition of the workers to the social and political omnipotence of the bourgeoisie, while it compels the admission that something more is needed than Trades Unions and strikes to break the power of the ruling class. But what gives these Unions and the strikes arising from them their real importance is this, that they are the first attempt of the workers to abolish competition.[63]

However, both men saw unions as contradictory organisations shaped both by their own particular function in society and, crucially, by the general political situation. The stress they put on the different sides of trades unions changed with the context. Most of their comments about unions come from the time of revolutionary ferment before 1848. Much of this focussed on the experience of Chartism in Britain. In the *German Ideology* of 1846, Marx had this to say about strikes and combinations:

> ...even a minority of workers who combine and go on strike very soon find themselves compelled to act in a revolutionary way – a fact [one] could have learned from the 1842 uprising in England and from the earlier Welsh uprising of 1839, in which year the revolutionary excitement among the workers first found comprehensive expression in the 'sacred month', which was proclaimed simultaneously with a general arming of the people.[64]

In the boom period that followed the defeat of the revolution, unions came to reflect more the sectionalism of industry.

During Marx and Engels' lifetime, union leaders also tended to become full-time bureaucrats, separated from the workforce, relatively comfortable and in regular contact with the bosses. Skilled union leaders in particular often became obsessed with battles and intrigues with other unions and union leaders. More generally, Marx and Engels recognised that the tendency was for unions to fight for and negotiate a better deal for workers within the system rather than to seek to overthrow it:

> Trade unions work well as centres of resistance against the encroachments of capital. They fail generally from limiting themselves to a guerrilla war against the effects of the existing system, instead of simultaneously trying to change it, instead of using their organised forces as a lever for the final emancipation of the working class, that is to say, the ultimate abolition of the wages system.[65]

Workers' political parties play a different role from that of the unions. Trade unions aim to recruit *all* workers in a particular industry to defend conditions. Socialist parties draw together workers with an existing commitment to wider social and political change in an effort to spread *specifically socialist ideas.* Marx and Engels advocated the creation of independent workers' parties in every country. This was a recognition of the fact that socialist ideas have to be campaigned and fought for amongst workers; that full class consciousness, though always a potential in capitalist society, is never automatic.

In the second half of the nineteenth century, however, creeping electoralism tended to reduce politics to what happened in parliament and had a corrupting influence on some labour leaders. Marx identified the dangers after the events of 1848 in France, when he wrote of 'a peculiar malady that after 1848 spread to a whole continent, *parliamentary cretinism* which confines its victim to an imaginary world and robs them of their senses, all recollection, all knowledge of the rude external world'.[66] The dangers became obvious in Britain too, where for many years, instead of proceeding 'at once to form a new a strong workers' party with a definite program', labour leaders looked to the votes and money of the bourgeoisie by trying to get on the Liberal Party ticket.[67]

Even when independent workers' parties were set up, the corrupting pressures of parliamentarianism remained. The German Social Democratic Party, which launched in 1863, was the biggest and strongest workers' party in the world. Its foundation marked a huge step forward in working-class organisation. But when Marx read its draft programme, he dashed off one of the fiercest polemics he ever wrote. For Marx the party's 'Gotha programme' promoted a confused politics of constitutionalism and rights rather than one based on self-activity and class struggle. It retained vague aspirations to abolish the wages system and 'an equal right to the undiminished proceeds of labour'. It argued however that change had to be worked for 'within the framework of the present-day national state' and that economic improvements would be handed down from above. As Marx commented in anger, the programme suggested that:

> Instead of being the result of the revolutionary process of social transformation in society, the socialist organisation of the whole of labour 'arises' from 'state aid' to producers' cooperative which the state, not the workers, is to call into being.[68]

For Marx, the Gotha programme showed the dangers of parliamentary socialist parties adapting to existing reality. It highlighted the risks of accepting the existing state and bending to the division of politics and economics built into capitalism's structure. The programme's practical proposals didn't go beyond demands that had already been introduced in other bourgeois states and its more general aspirations were not backed up with any strategy at all.

Marx and Engels never fully elaborated their ideas on workers' organisation. But the central thrust of their whole conception of the world was that socialism could only come through the self-activity, the active participation and struggle of workers and the conscious drawing of theoretical lessons from those struggles. As Engels put it in a later introduction to *The Communist Manifesto*, 'the emancipation of the working class must be the act of the working class itself'.[69] This was the principle that shaped their political and practice and their organising more than any other.

From the very start, Marx saw socialists' role not as trying to implement change or creating political programmes *on behalf* of workers but as struggling *alongside them* and at the same time clarifying the significance of their struggles. As he wrote explaining his new position to Ruge in 1843:

> We do not confront the world in a doctrinaire way with a new principle: Here is the truth, kneel down before it! We develop new principles for the world out of the world's own principles. We do not say to the world: Cease your struggles, they are foolish; we will give you the true slogan of struggle. We merely show the world what it is really fighting for, and consciousness is something that it has to acquire, even if it does not want to.[70]

These words, written before Marx had fully elaborated his ideas, capture very well the guiding spirit of what became Marx and Engels' political approach. The impetus for change comes from the struggle of working people. The role of socialists is to support individual struggles while at the same time generalising them, in the process developing the revolutionary consciousness and combativity of all those involved.

Their polemics show they were all too aware of the obstacles to change within the movement itself, as well as those created by class enemies. But Marx and Engels remained confident throughout their lives in the ability of working people to self-organise and ultimately destroy capitalist society. It was a capacity that they both glimpsed in numerous struggles, but more than any other in the seizure of Paris by working men and women in the months of the Commune of 1871. Marx's support for the commune may have made him the 'most slandered and most threatened man in London' but the actions of the working people of Paris and the changes they made filled him with joy:

When the Paris Commune took the management of the revolution in its own hands; when plain working men for the first time dared to infringe upon the governmental privilege of their 'natural superiors,' and, under circumstances of unexampled difficulty, performed their work modestly, conscientiously and efficiently, – performed it at salaries the highest of which barely amounted to one-fifth of what, according to high scientific authority, is the minimum required for a secretary to a certain metropolitan school-board – the old world writhed in convulsions of rage at the sight of the Red Flag, the symbol of the Republic of Labour, floating over the Hôtel de Ville.[71]

3. At Heaven's Gate

The decades after Marx's death in 1883 confirmed many of his ideas. Capitalism's extraordinary dynamism was borne out as industrial production spread across Europe, a good deal of the United States, parts of Russia and beyond. Imperial conquest brutally subordinated the majority of the globe to the main capitalist powers. In the process, the working class grew exponentially and new centres of working-class organisation developed around the world. Working-class militancy surged in the 1880s and 1890s and again before the First World War.

At the war's end, it exploded into a challenge to capitalism's survival. In Russia, the working class seized power, leading an alliance with the soldiers and the peasants, and sending shockwaves around the world. The idea that socialist theory could become a material force amongst workers had already been proved right by the rapid spread of socialist organisation from the last decades of the nineteenth century. On the other hand, as early as 1900, the majority of the socialist movement was showing signs of the kind of creeping accommodation with capitalism that had concerned both Marx and Engels towards the end of their lives.

However much historians try to downplay the importance of class, these developments decisively shaped early-twentieth-century history. The mid-nineteenth-century capitalist boom had ended in the 1870s as falling commodity prices and profits marked the beginning of a twenty-year depression. The capitalist class responded with a number of initiatives to restructure industry and restore profits. First, new technologies were developed and new sources of cheap labour were found in existing sectors. The search for new sources of profit led to a massive increase in investment in capital goods. This in turn led to competitive pressures and rapid technological innovation. In the context of growing imperial rivalry, the armaments industry became an important new sphere for profitable investment in the 1880s and 1890s, generating massive new industrial complexes, drawing in thousands of workers to a strategically sensitive industry and helping to encourage a lending spree to governments rushing to modernise and expand their armed forces.

These measures successfully restored the rate of profit. By the end of the nineteenth century, prices had started to rise faster than wages, unemployment grew and wealth was polarizing dramatically. The period from 1896 to the outbreak of the First World War has gone down in history as the 'belle époque', but for workers it was a time of rapid and traumatic change. First, the working class grew enormously. In Germany the number of industrial workers tripled from 1.8 million in 1873 to 5.7 million, or 22 per cent of the total labour force, in 1900.[72] By 1890, two-thirds of Americans worked for wages rather than owning a farm or business. By the turn of the century, industrial centres were emerging in Japan and Russia as well as in parts of eastern and southern Europe, drawing large numbers of agricultural workers into industry.

As a result, class structure was changing. New industries had generated new layers of unskilled workers and threatened craft standards, undermining the incorporation of skilled workers. Skilled workers began to reach out to the growing ranks of the unskilled. In Britain, this process led to the 'new unionism' of the late 1880s. In the four years after 1888, union membership doubled from 5 to 11 per cent of the workforce, with industrial unions in mining and transport leading the way. In the United States, union membership quadrupled between 1880 and 1890, and there was a surge in strikes from 1890. The strikes were frequently accompanied by marches from factory to factory through working-class neighbourhoods, calling for support. Beverly Silver gives a sense of how this insurgent dynamic played out:

The mushrooming size of the unskilled workforce and its concentration in downtown factory districts and working-class neighbourhoods facilitated both the rapid spread of protest across categories of workers and plants, and a growing common class consciousness. Protests launched in one plant or neighbourhood quickly spread, leading contemporary observers to use the epidemiological metaphor of 'contagious diseases' to describe the diffusion of protest.[73]

The spectacular growth of organised labour, its growing militancy and demands for electoral rights posed huge challenges for capitalists. The concentration of capital had already drawn the state more widely into economic and social affairs. New monopolies and cartels had emerged, demanding domestic support and back up in the pursuit of foreign interests. This integration found its most brutal expression in a new imperialist surge, in particular a horrific 'scramble for Africa'. Now the 'labour question' led to further demands for state intervention.

By the 1890s most European governments were widening the electorate and taking hesitant steps to limit the catastrophic impact of the free market on workers' lives. Social-insurance schemes of various sorts were pioneered in Germany and were spreading elsewhere by the turn of the century. Managements were recognising the existence of trade unions, which in many countries had rapidly expanding memberships and growing bureaucracies. This background of economic expansion and the promotion of nationalist and imperialist ideas profoundly shaped the emerging socialist movement.

The socialist challenge

Socialist parties from twenty countries had come together to form the Second International in Paris in 1889. Its congress opened on the centenary of the storming of the Bastille during the French revolution of 1789 and claimed direct lineage to the International Workingmen's Association in which Marx had been so influential. The hall was festooned with red flags and the closing words of *The Communist Manifesto*, 'Working men of all countries unite', were written in gold letters over the stage.[74]

The congress turned out to be the launchpad for spectacular growth in socialist organisation and influence, especially in Europe. Its leading component, the German Social Democratic Party (SPD), had polled 300,000 votes in a restricted vote in 1881. In 1912, the party went on to win four-and-half-million votes, 34 per cent of the total, and they claimed more than a million members by the outbreak of the First World War. The Italian Socialist Party won a quarter of votes cast and 78 deputies in 1913. The French party gained 102 seats in elections in 1914. Even in the USA, the Socialist Party polled 900,000 votes in 1912.[75]

Most of these parties claimed to be in the Marxist tradition and to stand for socialism, internationalism and against war. However, the fact that ruling classes were conceding to demands for electoral reform just as socialist ideas were winning a mass following in a number of countries had an impact. In practice, as Marx had feared, the parties' main focus was on winning elections. In Germany the ruling class at first did their best to keep the SPD out of the mainstream. The SPD responded to repression by creating something close to a state within a state. It had hundreds of different publications, affiliated trade unions and consumer groups, and a massive range of associations that related to every aspect of workers' lives. As one historian notes: 'No German town was without its democratic daily paper, its consumer cooperative, its workers' sports and cultural associations.'[76] The problem was that this immense apparatus, a model for parties in other countries, became an end in itself rather than a means to challenge the state.

Over time, the practice of electoralism and accommodation began to affect theory. The parties' gradualism found its first open expression at the end of the nineteenth century in the works of the SPD's leading theorist, Eduard Bernstein. From 1895, he began to argue that capitalism was overcoming its tendencies to crisis as monopolies and cartels suppressed competition. In his view, the growth of the state, the spread of share ownership and the widening of the franchise meant that revolution was both unlikely and unnecessary. Capitalism was creating the conditions in which workers could reform the system through the democratic process.

This open embrace of parliamentary politics involved a rejection of workers' capacities bordering on contempt:

> We cannot demand from a class the great majority of whose members live in crowded conditions, are badly educated, and have an uncertain and insufficient income, the high intellectual and moral standards which the organisation of and existence of a socialist community presupposes.[77]

Bernstein's revisionism brought him into conflict with those in the party who saw themselves as orthodox Marxists, particularly Karl Kautsky. The orthodox camp opposed Bernstein's reformism, saw capitalism as a crisis-ridden system and defended a revolutionary strategy for change. However, the position of Kautsky and his followers was also based on a fatalism foreign to Marx:

> We consider the breakdown of the present social system to be unavoidable, because we know that the economic evolution inevitably brings on conditions that will compel the exploited classes to rise against this system of private ownership.[78]

Kautsky's defence of Marxist orthodoxy sounds like the polar opposite of Bernstein's parliamentary policy. In fact, both led to the conclusion that change would come about through the spontaneous development of capitalism without decisive intervention from socialists. In Bernstein's case, this was because he thought capitalism was transforming itself, in Kautsky's it was because he thought it would inevitably collapse. Both views led to a passive attitude completely at odds with Marx's emphasis on self-activity and struggle.

There were important challenges to this drift to parliamentarianism and fatalism in working-class politics. In Germany itself, Rosa Luxemburg, Karl Liebknecht, Clara Zetkin and their supporters had been campaigning against the SPD's reformist direction for years. In 1900 Rosa Luxemburg published a brilliant polemic against revisionism. The pamphlet 'Reform or Revolution' remains one of the most eloquent cases for revolutionary politics. In it she argued that parliamentarism and revolution were not different paths to the same destination but two entirely different projects. Bernstein's revisionism was not in her view 'a more tranquil, slower road to the same goal' as revolution, it was a route to a different goal altogether. If we follow Bernstein's approach, she argued:

Our program becomes not the realisation of socialism, but the reform of capitalism; not the suppression of the wage labour system but the diminution of exploitation, that is, the suppression of the abuses of capitalism instead of suppression of capitalism itself.[79]

Despite her insistence that revolution could only be driven by mass activity of workers, her withering critique of Bernstein's revisionism and her rejection of fatalism, Luxemburg remained in the SPD up until 1916. She and her comrades continued to battle the opportunism of the right in the party. It was only when the SPD's capitulation to the war effort in 1914 made clear how deep the problem had become that they began to see the need to organise separately.

In Russia, Lenin and his supporters were developing a concept of socialist organisation very different from mainstream social democracy, but without being fully aware of the divergence. They split from others in the Russian Social Democratic Party in 1903, creating a long-term division between Lenin's Bolsheviks and the more moderate Mensheviks. The split appeared to some to be over a technicality, but it had important implications.

Like Luxemburg, Lenin prioritised working-class struggle over parliamentarianism. But he went further and drew important conclusions from the fact that there was a struggle *within* the working class over the ideas that dominated in the movement. In his discussion of the 1903 split Lenin questioned the notion that working-class opinion would gradually and inevitably grow into socialism as the social-democratic parties expanded. There were, Lenin recognised, 'differences in degree of consciousness and degree of activity' amongst workers.[80]

This had organisational implications. It meant that to be effective, to generate clarity and a genuinely revolutionary strategy, a socialist party had to organise the most revolutionary workers together into a vehicle which could then influence the rest of the class. As had been the case for Luxemburg, the experience of the 1905 revolution reinforced in Lenin a sense of the explosive potential of mass strikes and the organisation that flowed from it. But revolutionaries had a vital role. They had to distil the lessons of working-class struggle into a theory and practice that could be reinserted into contemporary battles. As he wrote in the midst of the events of 1905:

Undoubtedly, the revolution will teach us, and will teach the masses of the people. But the question that now confronts a militant political party is: shall we be able to teach the revolution anything?[81]

50

The dam breaks

These debates became critical in a matter of years. The first great insurgency of the twentieth century, the Russian revolution of 1905, was brutally crushed, but in the following years, class tensions rose pretty much everywhere. At the end of the First World War the questions of whether and how workers could change society and of how socialism could be achieved, suddenly became immediate, practical issues.

There was a huge spike in strike action in both the metropolitan countries and the colonial and semi-colonial worlds at the time. The most spectacular trade-union growth took place in Britain and the most violent class warfare outside Russia erupted in the United States, but on the eve of the war, strike levels were soaring in most even semi-industrialised countries. In country after country, there were mass strikes in the key sectors of mining, shipping and railways. Sectional differences were being overcome, 'absorbing unskilled, semi-skilled and skilled workers alike'.[82] In many places, strikes were taking on an insurgent and generalised character, causing acute anxiety in ruling circles.

The First World War, which began in 1914, was the catastrophic climax of mounting international competition for markets and resources. Ruling classes, however, hoped it might help on the home front. As the liberal historian A.J.P. Taylor put it, Europe's statesmen were convinced that 'war would stave off their social and political problems'.[83] For a time they were proved right. The start of the war exposed the extent to which socialist parties had accommodated to their national states. With the exceptions of both wings of the Russian party and the socialist organisations in Italy, Serbia and Romania, all the parties in belligerent countries backed their own government's war effort. Everywhere strikes ended and the majority of workers fell into line.

The war, however, only delayed and deepened social

crisis. The promise of a quick victory proved a delusion. Total war created hardship and shortages and required unheard of levels of coercion at the front and at home. As the body count moved into the millions, the sheer horror of the war fed growing opposition. The combination of carnage, economic chaos and repression blew away any lingering idea that the national democratic deal would deliver for workers. As a result, patriotic fervour turned into resistance and rebellion. In 1916 revolutionary socialists were amongst the leaders of the Easter rising against British rule of Ireland. Both French and British soldiers mutinied in 1917 and in Russia in February a revolution sparked by striking female factory workers brought down the Tsarist regime. Within days of the February Russian revolution, workers' and soldiers' councils had been established in the key cities and towns.

News of the Russian October Revolution later that year reverberated around the world and helped trigger the biggest surge of working-class struggle in history.[84] There were general strikes in Seattle and anti-colonial riots in India. The Austro-Hungarian Empire dissolved in waves of workers' revolt. There was a series of mass strikes in France as sailors, miners and engineers struck in sympathy with railway workers. In August 1917, female workers had already sparked four days of mass riots in Turin, demanding bread and peace.

The First World War was in fact ended by this wave of workers' revolution. The new regime in Russia had demanded an immediate peace over the heads of the enemy governments. Just over a year later, in November 1918, partly inspired by the Russian example, German sailors mutinied against a new offensive and sparked a working-class-led revolution in Germany that brought down the Kaiser and forced the German ruling class to sue for peace.

The German Revolution overthrew the monarchy but also put the question of workers' power in play. On the evening of the 9

November insurrection, hundreds of workers' representatives met in the great hall of the Reichstag, declaring themselves the provisional workers' and soldiers' council of the capital. They called for meetings in factories and garrisons the next day to elect delegates for a general assembly which would in turn appoint the new revolutionary government.[85] As workers' and soldiers' councils spread around the country, a panicked ruling class had to rely on the majority SPD leadership to contain workers' aspirations for fundamental change in the turmoil that followed.

The German Revolution gave new impetus to the revolutionary wave. A workers' republic was declared in 1919 in Hungary. 1919 and 1920 were dubbed 'the two red years' in Italy as huge factory occupations and the spread of factory councils raised the spectre of revolution. In Britain, police strikes and army mutinies in 1919 signalled the start of its deepest ever social crisis. Only the intervention of union leaders stopped a strike wave turning into a confrontation with the government in 1920 and 1921.[86]

Speaking at the 1919 Paris Peace conference, British Prime Minister David Lloyd George warned: 'Europe is in a revolutionary mood. The whole of the existing social, political and economic order is being called into question by the mass of people from one end of Europe to the other.'[87]

Practicing power

Russia was the only country in which workers took control for a significant period. As a result, the history of the Russian Revolution has become an ideological battleground. There is a whole academic industry devoted to proving that the October Revolution was a coup by a handful of conspirators rather than a takeover by workers. By trying to discredit the Russian Revolution, historians are attempting to deny the very possibility that workers can control society. This effort involves ignoring the extensive record of the mass participation that drove the revolutionary process. It is a record, however fleeting, that reveals the extraordinary creative and democratic potential unleashed when working people begin to take control of their own lives.

The great upsurge in working-class self-management and democratic control actually began immediately after the February revolution, six months before October. Soviets were established days after the overthrow of the Tsar and from that moment began to erode the power of the Russian state which was still in the hands of bourgeois forces. As a comprehensive study of the rank-and-file activity of the period concludes:

> Workers created a gamut of organizations and a huge variety of revolutionary practices that to some degree, constituted the embryo of a new social order. Not only was a national network of soviets set up, first by workers and soldiers and later by peasants, but also factory committees (probably the most important of the proletarian organizations), trade unions, workers' militias, Red Guards, consumer cooperatives, and educational and cultural organizations. Measured against this powerful grid of interlocking organizations, the Bolshevik party apparatus was puny...the Bolsheviks won support from the organizations by taking up their concerns as the party's own, and gradually rose to positions of leadership within the organizations, largely by democratic means.[88]

The soviets brought together directly elected representatives of the workers, the soldiers and, later, the peasants. Delegates from factories, regiments or villages were recallable. If they failed to reflect the positions of their electors, they could be and often were immediately replaced. Because they were rooted in the factories, the garrisons and the countryside, there was a direct, organic connection between decision making and the organised power at working-class centres. The new liberal government and the moderate Menshevik socialists did everything possible to limit the influence of the soviets, but the soviets remained the driving force of the revolution. As the Menshevik eyewitness Sukarnov wrote in frustration:

> The popularity and authority of the Soviet went on growing like a snowball amongst the urban and rural masses...not only in these masses but also in political circles and state institutions – there was taking root an awareness of the Soviet's real power and potentialities, and of the helplessness of the government and its agencies. The official government machine, in one part after another, began idling more and more. Independently of what either side desired, the official mechanism was being supplanted by the Soviet.[89]

By October key sections of the working class in Russia had come to see themselves as embodying the interests of the mass of society, exactly as Marx had predicted they would.[90] On the other hand, in a situation in which the bourgeois government refused to end the slaughter in the trenches, failed to deal with a desperate economic situation and was unable or unwilling to confront the growing threat of counter-revolution, the idea of workers' power appealed to wider and wider sections of the working class and to the most downtrodden. British journalist Morgan Philips Price, who was hostile to the Bolsheviks, was present at the Second Congress of the Soviets which took place at the very moment when workers seized power and declared the formation of the soviet state. He opposed the decisions made but couldn't hide his admiration for the sheer reach of soviet organisation into the working population, especially the poorest:

> Whole rows of benches were filled with sturdy, healthy

young men from the Baltic Fleet and from the front. The skilled artisans of Moscow and Petrograd, dressed in their collarless black shirts and with fur caps on their heads were also well to the fore. The peasant delegates were mostly young soldiers who had gone to their villages and taken the lead in the local communes...this Congress showed a preponderance of delegates from the northern and central provinces, the very districts in fact, where the largest number of poor, half proletarian peasants were found, where the skilled artisans dominated the towns and the hungry soldier deserters dominated the villages.[91]

Opening the session of the Petrograd soviet on the day of the revolution, Leon Trotsky declared that the bourgeois provisional government had ceased to exist. He noted too that despite the warnings of torrents of blood, the support for the revolution was so great that there had been no reports of any casualties, 'I don't know of any other example in history of a revolutionary movement involving such gigantic masses that was carried through without bloodshed.' He went on to underline the historic significance of the day:

At the present time, we, the Soviet of Soldiers, Workers' and Peasants' Deputies, are going to undertake an experiment unique in history, the establishment of a government that will have no other aim than the satisfaction of the needs of the soldiers, workers and peasants.[92]

A week after the revolution, a decree was issued giving all the peoples of Russia the right to free self-determination, up to secession and formation of independent states. Two decrees published in December 1917 swept aside the marriage and divorce laws and demanded full equality for the sexes. They recognised only civil marriage; children born out of wedlock were given the same rights as the offspring of marriage; divorce was to be had for the asking by either spouse. Meanwhile, all the judges of the old regime were sacked, the complete separation of church from state and school was made law in February 1918 and any existing legislation that contradicted the revolutionary decrees was declared invalid. This extraordinary programme could be not implemented from above. It was taken up in extremely difficult circumstances by workers and peasants across the country as they extended their control of the factories and proceeded to break up the great estates.

Explaining isolation

Outside Russia, capitalism weathered the post-war revolutionary storm. By 1921, the immediate crisis had been contained and the Russian Revolution stood isolated, a situation that its leaders knew was unsustainable. Many explanations of this situation focus on an apparently exceptional set of circumstances in Russia which made it uniquely vulnerable to revolution. The ruling classes at the time had no such sense of certainty. The moderate socialist historian Gaetano Salvemini, for example, wrote the following about the crisis in Italy in 1920 and the role of the left trade union the CGL and the Italian Socialist Party (PSI):

> If the leaders of the CGL and the PSI had wanted to strike a decisive blow, they had the opportunity. The bankers, the big industrialists, the big landowners, were waiting for the socialist revolution like a ram waits to be led to the slaughterhouse.[93]

The German Revolution too was profoundly threatening to the capitalist order. Its great historian, Pierre Broué, makes the case that there was in fact more possibility of a soviet-based outcome in the German Revolution in November 1918 than there had been in Russia in February 1917. 'Despite the weakness of their organisation,' he argues, 'the German revolutionaries played a more important role in the formation of the councils than the Bolsheviks did in the formation of the soviets.'[94] Unlike in the Russian February Revolution, revolutionaries in Germany led some of the most important workers' councils and the SPD were desperately scrambling to re-establish control in the first weeks of the revolution. That they eventually did so was a product more than anything of their organisational strength and their resulting influence in the key sections of the working class.[95]

There is another problem with the idea of Russian exceptionalism; it relegates the question of working-class consciousness and organisation to an afterthought. One of the things that was unique about Russia was that there was an openly revolutionary organisation there with real influence amongst workers. The Bolshevik Party had had years to sink roots into the Russian working class and, though it had only had minority support in February 1917, its role over the following months was central. The soviets drew together the great mass of working people and so reflected overall opinion in the class.

In the months immediately after February the political approach proposed by the moderate Mensheviks dominated. Menshevik influence was, however, broken down over time through a combination of workers' own experience and the alternative political approach proposed by the Bolsheviks. Where the Mensheviks tried to limit the power of the soviets and return to parliamentary politics, the Bolsheviks famously demanded 'all power to the soviets'. Where the Mensheviks called vaguely for a negotiated peace, the Bolsheviks demanded an immediate ceasefire. When right-wing forces under General Kornilov tried to crush the revolution, the Bolsheviks proved energetic leaders of a workers' resistance while the Mensheviks prevaricated. As October approached and it became clear that a majority in the soviets had become convinced of the need for a second revolution, the Bolsheviks were organising and agitating for it while the Mensheviks opposed it right up until the day it happened.

At the start of the war, the kind of independent revolutionary organisation pioneered by the Bolsheviks did not exist outside of Russia. Pierre Broué argues that the failure of the German revolutionaries to break from social democracy earlier and build an explicitly revolutionary current inside the working class cost the left dearly:

> What was lacking in the German soviets in 1918 was the concerted activity of patient explanation which the Bolsheviks carried on in Russia, which enabled them to strengthen the soviets and their authority between February and October, and to win the majority in the soviets so that they could become a weapon in the struggle for power.[96]

In Italy too there was something approaching a revolutionary crisis but no revolutionary organisation. Despite a spreading movement of factory occupations and growing calls for the seizure of power, union leaders refused to organise an insurrection. They offered to stand aside and hand over their positions if the leaders of the Italian Socialist Party wanted to organise the revolution. They in turn declined the offer on the grounds that they couldn't do it without the union leaders. The result was that the revolution was postponed indefinitely. As Schiavello, a left-wing trade unionist, commented bitterly at the following Socialist Party convention:

> We have been subjected to a fait accompli; perhaps we wanted it, perhaps we did not. We lack organization. We lack a party that can capture the spirit of the people. We lack a party which does not live divided, with two different souls. We lack the iron hand. Maybe we lack a communist party comrades![97]

The victory of the Russian Revolution and the inadequacies of the social-democratic parties internationally created a deep crisis in the working-class movement. The Russian Communists launched the Third International in 1919 on the basis of a clear distinction between revolutionary and reformist politics. In the years that followed, Communist parties were formed around the world attracting many of the most militant working-class activists. More turmoil followed. Germany was shaken by a new revolutionary crisis in 1923, Britain by a general strike in 1926 and the Chinese ruling class faced a very serious working-class insurgency in 1927. In 1933, France's working class occupied factories and workplaces in a militant response to the election of a left-wing government. In 1936, the Spanish working class rose up and fought an insurgent civil war against Franco's fascist attack on the popular-front government. In all these cases, new opportunities for change opened up.

From the second half of the 1920s, however, a new dynamic had developed in the global socialist movement. The isolation of the Russian revolution had taken its toll, as the Bolshevik leaders always warned it would. Russia had been besieged by imperialist armies after the revolution and though the Red Army won the civil war, the cost was immense. The working class had been devastated by war, famine and economic collapse. The major cities were depopulated as workers were forced to scour the countryside for food. By the time of Lenin's death in 1924, the output of Russia's factories was still below that of 1914. The vibrant soviet democratic culture lay broken in the ruins.

In these desperate circumstances, Stalin was able to concentrate power in his own hands around the call for socialism in one country. What lay behind that call and the repression that followed was a complete break with Leninism and the principles of the revolution. The consolidating Stalinist bureaucracy forced through economic development in Russia by massively stepping up the exploitation of the Russian working class.[98]

The Stalinist counter-revolution was first and foremost a catastrophe for the Russian working class, but it had disastrous implications for the workers' movement internationally. From the mid-1920s, the policy promoted by the Communist International reflected first the twists and turns of Stalin's domestic policy as he fought to consolidate his power, and then his assessment of the Soviet Union's international interests as it manoeuvred for power on the world stage. After an ultra-left period, Stalinist international policy took a turn in 1935 towards cooperating with 'progressive bourgeois' forces against the growing threat of fascism. The Spanish Communist Party fatally smothered the revolutionary energy of the movement in an alliance with those bourgeois parties that opposed the Franco coup. Everywhere the interests of workers were subordinated to the narrow concerns of the Russian bureaucracy.

Revolutionary reflections

The years that followed the First World War provided a mass of new experience for socialists to process. The period remains the highpoint of revolutionary history, and the debates it generated about class, consciousness and organisation continue to resonate. In the years that followed, three major works attempted to synthesise the revolutionary experience and draw out some of its most essential lessons.

One was Leon Trotsky's *History of the Russian Revolution*. After Lenin's death in 1924, Leon Trotsky led the struggle against the degeneration of the Russian Revolution. Trotsky fought Stalin on many fronts and one of them was the interpretation of the revolution itself. His massive history runs to half a million words and remains the great defence and analysis of that experience and one of the most important pieces of history writing of any period. It situates the revolution in its broad historical sweep but also examines in detail the interplay between spontaneous struggle, the moods of different strata in society and conscious political intervention that forged the revolution. *The History of the Russian Revolution* is an absolutely unparalleled examination of the real-world mechanisms of self-organisation and of the relationship between revolutionary struggle and the nature of workers' power.

Trotsky's narrative illustrates again and again Marx and Engel's view of insurrection as an art. In Trotsky's own words, it is an art which 'presupposes a correct general leadership of the masses, a flexible orientation in changing conditions, a thought out plan of attack, cautiousness in technical preparation, and a daring blow'.[99] The central feature of the revolution for Trotsky was 'the forcible entrance of the masses into the realm of rulership over its own destiny'.[100] Trotsky, however, went on to argue that there is an important difference between socialist and bourgeois revolutions. In the transition to capitalism, emerging capitalist relations were able at least partly to erode feudal relations from within. Because this option isn't open to workers and because of the way capital dominates social relations in modern society, a relatively impulsive upsurge of popular struggle will never be enough to overcome capitalism. For this an extremely high level of consciousness, strategy and organisation is necessary. As he put it:

> The dynamic of revolutionary events is directly determined by swift, intense and passionate changes in the psychology of classes which have already formed themselves before the revolution. However the spontaneous activity of the masses is not sufficient for the victory of the revolution. Without a mass revolutionary party, victory for the proletariat is not possible. Without a guiding organisation, the energy of the masses would dissipate like steam not enclosed in a piston-box. But nevertheless what moves things is not the piston or the box, but the steam.[101]

The difference between the February and the October revolutions illustrates the point. In February, the Tsarist order was overthrown by a relatively spontaneous mass movement (although even here Trotsky makes the point that socialist activists played an important galvanising role). Such a movement was not, however, capable of preventing the power grab by a provisional government that had capitalist interests at its heart.

The October Revolution, the actual seizure of power by workers, was different. It could only take place in a situation in which the majority of workers, soldiers and millions of peasants understood its nature and necessity and were prepared to participate. It involved careful planning and the conscious deployment of forces from below to knock out various centres of state power and to seize control of key installations and workplaces. It involved above all a permanent mobilisation of working people in democratic institutions that would begin to run society in a new way.

In his history of the revolution, and in the years that followed, Trotsky stressed another crucial aspect of socialist organising that has received less attention than his insistence on the need for a revolutionary party. Workers' instinctive, practical consciousness often runs ahead of the development of a fully worked-out worldview. As a result, loyalty to existing organisations dies hard. For these reasons, it is important for revolutionaries to work together with other groups of workers who remain under the influence of more moderate organisations. This involved the strategy that Trotsky and Lenin had called 'the united front'.

In the 1930s, for example, Trotsky insisted that revolutionaries in Germany should bloc with the reformist socialists in an active alliance against the rise of Hitler's Nazis. Trotsky wasn't asking the communists to drop their political differences with the social democrats, he was simply demanding that they make a practical agreement to struggle together against fascism. In circumstances in which the fascists were attempting 'to encircle the revolutionary strongholds', to oppose working with the social democrats on principle was 'to give direct and immediate aid to fascism'.[102] In the process of mounting a successful united campaign the leaders of social democracy would be tested, and the revolutionary policy vindicated.

For Trotsky, the united front was not simply a short-term, tactical response to an emergency. The need for revolutionaries to unite with other working-class forces, without dropping their politics or abandoning their organisation, was dictated by the nature of class consciousness under capitalism. Even in revolutionary times when the overwhelming majority of the working class recognise the need to unite and change the existing regime, he argued that:

This does not mean, however, that they all understand how to do it, and still less that they are ready at the very moment to break with their parties and to join the ranks of the communists. The political conscience of the class does not mature so methodically and so uniformly; deep inner divergences remain even in the revolutionary epoch when all processes develop by leaps and bounds.[103]

It was for this reason that Trotsky insisted that soviets or workers' councils were an indispensable element in any successful revolution. They were 'the highest form of the united front', the ultimate expression of working-class unity at a time when the need for 'an organisation above parties and embracing the entire class becomes extremely urgent'.[104]

Two other revolutionaries, the Italian Antonio Gramsci and the Hungarian Georg Lukács, made original theoretical contributions on the basis of the experience of the years of revolution. Gramsci's *Prison Notebooks* and Lukács' *History and*

Class Consciousness both focussed on the relationship between class and class consciousness in advanced capitalist society. They sought to analyse and explain both the dramatic surge in workers' struggle after the First World War, and the mechanisms by which it had been contained.

The Italian Communist Party leader Gramsci had been arrested and thrown into prison by Mussolini's fascist government in 1926. There he wrote a series of notebooks exploring problems of class consciousness and revolutionary strategy in more advanced capitalist countries. Building on Marx, one of Gramsci's central insights was that at all times, workers had a contradictory consciousness, generated on the one hand by their immediate experience of work and struggle, and the ideas circulating in society on the other:

> One might almost say that he (the worker) has two theoretical consciousnesses (or one contradictory consciousness): one which is implicit in his activity and which in reality unites him with all his fellow workers in the practical transformation of the real world; and one, superficially explicit or verbal, which he has inherited from the past and uncritically absorbed.[105]

To explain workers' acceptance of the system most of the time, Gramsci emphasised the role of the complex network of civil-society institutions in modern capitalism: the media, the education system, the civil service, religious organisations and so on. All of these had the effect not just of promoting ideologies hostile to the working class, but actively incorporating workers into alien institutions. Consent also flows from the ruling classes' general dominance and control of society, especially their control of production:

> The 'spontaneous' consent given by the great masses of the population to the general direction imposed on social life by

the dominant fundamental group...is 'historically' caused by the prestige (and consequent confidence) which the dominant group enjoys because of its position and function in the world of production.[106]

Sustaining this consent then depends on the ruling classes' ability to take society forward. Because capitalism is a contradictory and crisis-ridden system, this is far from guaranteed. In periods of turmoil, the careful balance which ruling classes seek between consent and coercion can break down and create the conditions for a 'crisis of authority'. This was exactly the situation which developed after the First World War, 'in the period following the World War, cracks opened up everywhere in the hegemonic apparatus, and the exercise of hegemony became permanently difficult'.[107]

Whether or not the working class understands and takes advantage of such moments of destabilisation depended for Gramsci on a number of things. The first prerequisite was a level of collective resistance. It is when workers act and struggle as a group that they develop their own 'embryonic' understanding of the world. Even then, understanding develops 'occasionally and in flashes'. Secondly, socialist organisation was needed to help turn those flashes into a more sustained illumination which can reveal the path forward. Echoing Marx's words to Ruge, Gramsci argued it was not socialists' job to invent a new programme, or to introduce 'from scratch a scientific form of thought'. Working-class struggle itself begins to break down ruling-class ideas and prejudices, and raises the possibility of a more coherent worldview. Socialists' task is one of 'renovating and making "critical" an already existing activity' or, as he wrote later, making 'coherent the principles and the problems raised by the masses in their practical activity'.[108]

This is a model of revolutionary organisation which is worlds away from the passive electoralism of the parties that had dominated the Second International. It was a reassertion of Marx's insight that struggle is the key not just to social change but to understanding the world. It also acknowledged that spontaneous struggle on its own would not lead to full class consciousness because old ideas live on in people's minds alongside the new. This model involved operating alongside workers at the frontline of the struggle, helping to identify the next practical steps and linking immediate battles with the wider struggle for change, while all the time drawing out the broader theoretical lessons.

Finally, in the *Notebooks*, Gramsci rejects the sectarianism that bedevilled the early Italian Communist Party. Again and again, he stresses the need for the revolutionary elements of the working class to place themselves at the centre of wider alliances in its struggle for power. Sometimes this has been misinterpreted as an abandonment of a revolutionary strategy in favour of a 'long march through the institutions'.[109] In fact in the *Notebooks*, Gramsci recognises the united front advocated by Lenin and Trotsky as the key to undermining the ruling-class power and influence in the more complex, integrated states of the West. The task of creating an effective challenge to capitalist control involves providing leadership to other oppressed groups and building alliances with workers and others who haven't yet fully absorbed the lessons of the crisis:

> The proletariat can become the leading and ruling class to the extent to which it succeeds in creating a system of class alliances which enables it to mobilise the majority of the working population against capitalism and the bourgeois state.[110]

Whereas Gramsci's analysis tended to operate at the level of institutions and ideas in society, the Hungarian revolutionary Georg Lukács grounded his analysis of class consciousness in capitalism's economic processes. While Lukács' analyses were often less concrete than Gramsci's, this connection to capitalism's underlying structure gave them exceptional explanatory power.[111] Lukács built on Marx's ideas about the ideological impact of alienation. The robbery involved in exploitation removed from workers any control over the process of production or their own working lives. Production was fragmented by the division of labour and appeared to be driven by the vagaries of the market rather than human need.

> Neither objectively nor in his relation to his work does man appear as the authentic master of the process: On the contrary he is a mechanical part incorporated into a mechanical system. He finds it already pre-existing and self-sufficient, it functions independently of him and he has to conform to its laws whether he likes it or not.[112]

One important result of alienation was that real relationships involved in production and circulation are hidden by an apparently given and fragmented world of objects and measurements. Following Marx, Lukács called the way commodity production appeared to turn processes and relations into things, 'reification'. Lukács however advanced some way beyond Marx, by stressing the extent to which this process of reification affects the whole of society, not just the core capitalist work process. All aspects of the state, the justice system, the civil service and so on, end up functioning with the same formal, quantitative, standardised laws, which deny people their humanity and individuality by treating them as abstract individuals.

Democracy itself is profoundly shaped by these processes. We have seen that civil society under capitalism is subject to a 'division of labour' in which economic and fundamental social questions are separated from politics. Lukács showed, however, that by treating us all as equals, as consumers, as citizens, as electors, this system of rights and democracy which extends across society helps to conceal the fact that the whole edifice rests on the domination of one class over another. This atomisation of politics 'pulverises bourgeois society politically' and inhibits the development of independent politics among workers and the oppressed which could genuinely correspond to their own class interests.

Lukács was not, however, just concerned to show how capitalism *distorts* workers' consciousness as so many radical thinkers have done since. Lukács also explained how the system generates resistance and radicalisation. The capitalists, Lukács showed, have one central problem. Turning labour power into a commodity creates an issue for the bosses because workers, unlike any other commodity, have a personality and a consciousness. Henry Ford was bemoaning this situation when he complained, 'why is it every time I ask for a pair of hands, they come with a brain attached?'[113] When bosses respond to market pressures by trying to force down wages, lengthen the working day or cut meal breaks, this particular commodity tends to object and often resist. The opposition normally starts as partial: a sectional struggle against a pay cut, a change of contract or redundancies. The outbreak of a dispute over pay or conditions at work is destabilising in itself, but it is also a demonstration that the logic of commodification, the fragmented rationality of market forces, hides a deeper, more antagonistic process.

Once workers organise and resist and begin to overcome passivity, some of the mysteries surrounding commodification start to evaporate. It becomes clear that what appeared to be the impersonal logic of the market is in fact a set of repressive relations between people based on the ownership of production by a tiny minority:

Now that this core is revealed it becomes possible to recognise the fetish character of every commodity based on the commodity character of labour power: in every case we find its core, the relation between men, entering into the evolution of society.[114]

The great struggles after the First World War had proved that when class struggle erupts on a large scale it tends to lead to sudden shifts in class consciousness. The impact of class struggle has the effect of revealing workers' power and importance in society. The need for solidarity clarifies who is with the workers and who is against them. Intense class struggle draws in key institutions and in the process begins to expose the fiction of the independence of the police, the courts, the media and other arms of the state. As a result, the most active workers at least start to generate a realistic picture of the power relations in capitalist society. When workers start to recognise their own status as commodities as a result of these kind of struggles, they can begin to understand the nature of the whole society based on commodification.

Lukács, then, was elaborating Marx's insight that working-class struggle was not just the most effective way for workers to win improvements in their lives, but the key to gaining an understanding of the nature of the system. In this sense, workers' position in society gives them a unique vantage point from which to grasp the contours of capitalist society:

(T)he knowledge of reality provided by the dialectical method is likewise inseparable from the class standpoint of the proletariat...For, the Marxist method, the dialectical materialist knowledge of reality, can arise only from the point of view of the struggle of the proletariat.[115]

This, however, is not the end of the story. The experience of the struggles after the Russian Revolution taught Lukács that spontaneous struggles only take people so far. In times of social crisis, mass strikes can take on aspects of a civil war, but even in such moments, lessons have to be made conscious, organisation is needed to express and embody them and to take struggle forward. Because of the inevitable unevenness within the working class and the dead hand of reification, even in times of crisis, workers' organisations will be shaped partly by the reality of capitalist life.

The result is that even in periods of acute crisis, 'in many respects the proletariat is still caught up in the old capitalist forms of thought and feeling'.[116] Trade unions, for example, are the basic unit of working-class resistance but also reflect some of the existing divisions amongst workers between different industries and different grades. However important they are to workers' self-defence and to developing combativity, their aims are limited to winning the best possible deal for workers within the existing society. They don't extend to fundamentally changing it. The reformist parties on the other hand end up trying to ensure that workers' *politics* doesn't develop beyond the bounds of bourgeois ideals, doesn't challenge the basis of private property or push for the democratisation of the workplace and therefore the economy. This is why, in order to capitalise on moments of opportunity, specifically revolutionary organisation is necessary.

4. The Myth of Class Compromise

In the years between the end of the Second World War and the late 1960s, it appeared to some that class antagonisms were vanishing in a world of mass abundance. The system experienced a record, almost uninterrupted economic boom from the mid-1940s to the end of the 1960s. It seemed to be overcoming the contradictions that had almost brought it down between the wars. In Britain, the Labour politician and intellectual Anthony Crossland put the case most effectively in his 1956 bestseller *The Future of Socialism*. The divided society, he argued, was evolving into something brave and new:

> Poverty and insecurity are in the process of disappearing. Living standards are rising rapidly; the fear of unemployment is steadily weakening; the ordinary young worker has hopes that would never have entered his father's head.[117]

The result was that, 'It is manifestly inaccurate to call Britain a capitalist society.'[118]

In the US, elite sociologists had launched an intellectual rearguard action in the 1930s, which involved writing class struggle out of the study of society. Harvard's Talcott Parsons led the way arguing that society was divided into 'strata' rather than classes and that stratification was grounded in social values rather than in any economic reality.[119] By the mid-1950s, in the middle of the boom, sociologist Daniel Bell could go further, announcing the 'end of ideology'. He described the emergence of a world in which there was no longer a recognisable elite and in which politics 'is not a reflection of any class division'. Capitalism itself had made possible the 'organisation of production, control of inflation and maintenance of full employment'.[120]

In politics, a consensus emerged that capitalism's tendency to conflict and crisis could be overcome if governments intervened modestly in the economy in the way advocated by John Maynard Keynes in the 1930s. Keynes had argued that state intervention could overcome boom and bust, and ensure something approaching full employment across the business cycle. Around the world during the boom, most social-democratic parties dropped the language of class and embraced the view that, with the help of limited state intervention, capitalism would grow over into a more rational and fairer system. Mild Keynesianism often morphed into a straightforward celebration of corporate capitalism's achievements. Labour's 1957 policy statement *Industry and Society* echoed Crossland's themes, arguing that nationalisation was unnecessary because 'Under increasingly professional managements, large firms are as a whole serving the nation well.'[121] The German Social Democratic Party explicitly rejected class politics at its 1959 Bad Godesburg conference. Other European parties were on a similar trajectory, if at different speeds.[122]

Even some self-proclaimed Marxists embraced the idea that capitalism could be rationalised. By the 1950s, for example, the most popular British Marxist writer of the 1930s, John Strachey, was arguing that Keynes had been right and that capitalism's tendency to crisis could be reformed away by energetic government action.[123] Other radicals echoed these ideas by adopting the view that the working class had been effectively bought off or absorbed by ascendant capitalism. Theorising a growing strand of third worldism in the 1960s, the American Marxists Paul Baran and Paul Sweezey accepted that the working class in the West had been successfully incorporated and argued that the post-colonial regimes were the major remaining threat to capitalism. Meanwhile, the critical US sociologist C. Wright Mills argued that students had taken on the mantle of radical change abandoned by the working class.

The basic interpretation of the period has proved enduring even on the left. The standard left social-democratic view remains that state intervention did indeed overcome many of capitalism's irrationalities and excesses and that it was abandoning statism in the 1970s that led to the return of crisis and austerity. The Marxist 'regulation' school of economists argued that during the boom a 'Fordist' deal between big corporations and workers had insured that workers' wages were high enough to consume ever-increasing output.[124] More recently, Gerard Dumenil and Dominique Levy have argued that post-war growth was a product of a Keynesian approach which involved a 'compromise' between industrial capital and the organised working class.[125] David Harvey concurs that the post-war years saw a 'compromise between capital and labour' in which Keynesian policies were successfully used to dampen business cycles and ensure near full employment.[126] Wages and standards of living for working people did rise steadily for most of the three decades following the war. In many countries of 'advanced capitalism', the period was marked by the transformation of punitive poor laws into a more generous welfare state, the establishment of centralised, state-run, free systems of education, the clearing of slums to make way for planned housing schemes and the emergence of a domestic economy that allowed workers some access to a range of consumer goods and commercial entertainment. The boom years were a period of relative social calm in which demands for radical change were forced to the margins.

Nevertheless, the conventional wisdom that the period can be defined by transformation through state intervention and class compromise is wrong on several counts. It is challenged first by the explosion of insurgent class struggle that began towards the end of the Second World War. Far from being the outcome of a new spirit of class collaboration, 'the post-war settlement' was built on the defeat and containment of this upsurge. Secondly, the idea that the boom was the result of the permanent suppression of capitalism's irrationalities, either through its own evolution or state intervention, simply proved false. The boom ended, and mostly it ended on the watch of Keynesian regimes. While it was on, it was sustained by a high rate of profit which emerged before the planning craze. Thirdly, as a matter of fact, exploitation, class division and class struggle continued in the developed and the developing world throughout the period. In particular, despite the caricatures of 1968, class struggle was at the centre of the social explosions that marked the boom time's end.

Riding the storm

In his memoirs, Winston Churchill described a discussion he had with Stalin about the post-war future of the Balkans in 1944:

I wrote out on half a sheet of paper:

Rumania: Russia 90 percent, the others 10 percent
Greece: Great Britain 90 percent (in accord with USA), Russia 10 percent
Yugoslavia: 50-50 percent
Hungary: 50-50 percent
Bulgaria: Russia 75 percent, the others 25 percent
I pushed this across to Stalin, who had by then heard the translation.
There was a slight pause. Then he took his blue pencil and made a large tick upon it, and passed it back to us. It was all settled in no more time than it takes to set down.[127]

These notes clearly didn't correspond exactly to outcomes, but they give a sense of the spirit of the great power carve up of Europe and beyond at the end of the war. At the key conferences of Yalta and Potsdam, the US aimed to impose its leadership on Western

Europe and to extend its influence elsewhere by challenging the European formal empires. Britain was desperate to hold on to as many of its imperial possessions as it could and Stalin wanted to maintain control of the Balkans and as much of Eastern Europe as possible. To achieve these aims, Stalin was happy to participate in the carve up. Fatefully, his key leverage was control of the communist parties outside of the Soviet sphere.

As well as realpolitik, the initial post-war co-operation between the leaders of the great powers was driven by anxiety that the situation could slip out of their control.

The Second World War had led to death, destruction and trauma on an industrial scale and it brought to a head anger at the political establishments which had presided over political and economic failure for decades. Across a good deal of Europe, Eastern and Western elites had lost all legitimacy by collaborating with the losing, Nazi-led alliance. In many European countries, popular resistance movements had played a key role in uprooting fascist or fascist-supporting governments. In the colonial world, participation in the war accelerated pressure for independence. The result was that millions of people were looking for solutions outside traditional political options. In the words of one of the great historians of the Second World War:

> Wherever the Anglo-American armies went, those traditional classes and elements with whom their leaders were most inclined to align themselves were fatally discredited politically and morally, far weaker than at any time in recent history and irreversibly compromised in the face of the Resistance forces that were mushrooming to challenge them, movements that now possessed a unique claim to the mantle of nationalist legitimacy.[128]

The post-war settlement depended then not just on the military outcome but also on a struggle between the elites of the victorious powers and these social forces, mainly made up of workers and peasants, groping for fundamental change. In France in 1944 as Allied troops fought their way south there were mass uprisings in many key industrial towns. Fascist authorities were cleared away by popular militia groups and Liberation committees were set up to fill the administrative vacuum. These committees took control of the process of 'epuration', the purging from positions of power and often execution of fascist supporters. In a country whose bourgeoisie had largely collaborated with the Nazi occupation, the epuration was a clear threat to continued class rule. Particularly in the industrial centres of Lyons and Marseille and the surrounding area, workers' committees, often led by Communist Party members, took direct control of purged industries.[129] Re-imposing the broken capitalist state in the face of these movements was the main challenge facing the French ruling class and their allied backers.

In Italy too, workers and the left were central to driving out the fascists and their supporters. As one recent account of Italian women's role in the anti-fascist struggle describes, in Turin, Italy's biggest industrial city, the fascists had been driven out or into hiding by the time the Allies arrived:

> When the first Allied soldiers, a small group of Americans in jeeps, entered Turin on 30 April, they found the traffic lights working, the shops open, the trams running, the streets swept and the people walking calmly about. Many of them sported red handkerchiefs, as if, noted an onlooker somewhat sourly, 'they had all fought with the partisans'. Bunches of flowers and sometimes photographs were lying where the partisans had died.[130]

The northern partisans' success was driven more than anything by the action of organised workers. By March 1944 about half a million workers were taking co-ordinated strike action across the north in which economic and political demands were united.[131] The liberation was accompanied by the formation of workers' committees to run the factories in Milan and Turin. As a result of its central role in these struggles the Italian Communist Party grew from 5000 members in June 1943 to a staggering 1.7 million members two years later.[132] No wonder then that immediately after liberation, Lt Col. Stevens, the British Officer in charge of Allied missions, was lecturing Italian politicians in the north 'on the need to bring the partisans firmly into line, obedient to the Allies and under military control'.[133]

European class struggle reached its highest pitch in Greece. The country's National Liberation Front (EAM), which had a strong Communist Party component, had played the key role in defeating the Nazi armies by October 1944. At liberation it had around two million members out of a total population of a little over seven million and claimed to control three-quarters of the country's territory. Workers had begun to assert control, including taking over factories in urban centres. Greece was part of Britain's sphere of influence, and Churchill decided to send in large numbers of troops at the end of 1944 to stop popular forces from taking control. A banned demonstration in Athens gave him the pretext to attack the left and the Battle of Athens began. Churchill's guidance to British generals was clear:

...do not hesitate to fire at any armed male in Athens who assails the British authority or Greek authority with which we are working. It would be well of course if your commands were reinforced by the authority of some Greek government...Do not however hesitate to act as if you were in a conquered city where a local rebellion is in progress.[134]

This phase of the war ended with the disarmament of the EAM's armed wing and the transfer of the majority of the country to the control of the British-backed Athens regime. At least 50,000 members of the resistance were interned.

There were insurgencies in the East too. The people of Warsaw rose up against the Nazi occupation on 1 August 1944. For 63 days, until it was crushed, Poland's capital was under popular control. The demands of the uprising's leadership included:

Agrarian reform covering estates of over 50 hectares... Socialization of key industries...Participation of workers in the management of enterprises and control by workers of industrial production.[135]

After the military defeat of the Nazi armies there were revolutionary upsurges in three of the Eastern European countries that had allied with Germany: Bulgaria, Hungary and Romania. The revolutionary mood reached its highest level in Bulgaria where according to *The Economist* magazine, the army itself had gone over to the revolution, in scenes that recalled the picture of the Russian Army in 1917: 'Soldiers' councils have been set up, officers have been degraded, red flags hoisted, and normal saluting abolished.'[136]

The great wave of protest and class struggle continued in many places for a number of years after the war but was in the end successfully contained. Partly this was a result of physical repression on both sides of the East/West divide. Crucially, most governments undertook programmes of nationalisation and in the West, many rolled out extensive reform schemes in housing, education, health care, urban recreation and leisure, all based on redistributive taxation. These reforms went some way towards meeting the aspirations of working classes radicalised by the experience of the slump and war.

They were partly sustained by the massive injection of funds by the US government in the Marshall aid plan from 1948, which helped reboot broken European economies and promote 'safe' governments. The political purpose of US funding for Europe was not a secret. In March 1947, US President Truman asked Congress for $400 million dollars to fight against communist influence in Greece and Turkey, for instance. It is important to recognise that social reform of these years was largely driven by the fear of insurgent working-class action.[137] As early as 1940, the British Minister of Food and later of Reconstruction, Lord Woolton, wrote in his diary that without rapid post-war rebuilding, 'There will be both the tendency and the excuse for revolution.'[138] Three years later the Tory MP Quintin Hogg was even blunter, telling parliament, 'If you do not give them social reforms, they will give you social revolution.'[139]

Given the influence of the communist parties, however, the relative stabilisation of the situation couldn't have happened without their co-operation. At the end of the war, Russia's control over international communist policy was absolute and that policy was to be determined entirely by the Russian bureaucracy's foreign interests. The first task was the defeat of the Nazi armies, the second was to sustain friendly relations with the Western powers. This meant full co-operation with bourgeois governments and strict opposition to all revolutionary initiatives. Stalin hoped that the suppression of class demands by the communist parties would engender trust in Russia by its allies so that they could continue to work together after the war.[140] The Soviets made no bones about it. Former Foreign Minister Maxim Litvinov assured the American representative on the Italian Advisory Committee in September 1944: "We do not want revolutions in the West".[141]

Despite its leading role in liberation committees and the popular militias, and to widespread dismay from the rank and file, the French Communist Party's leaders agreed both to them being wound up and to workers being disarmed.[142] Returning to Paris from Moscow in February 1944, the leader of the Party,

Maurice Thorez, insisted on joining a government led by the right-winger Charles de Gaulle and that all authority should be placed back in the hands of the state. His policy was summed up in the slogan 'One state, one army, one police force'.[143]

The Italian Communist Party leader Palmiro Togliatti worked with the Allied authorities to disarm the partisans and was lukewarm towards the Socialist Party's plan for a complete purge of fascists.[144] In a famous press conference at Salerno on 1 April 1944, Togliatti agreed to join a government headed by former fascist general Badoglio, accepted that the question of abolishing the collaborationist monarchy should be put off until the end of the war and committed to working towards class co-operation in a parliamentary Italy.[145] As early as August 1943, the leadership of the Greek party had accepted that 'Greece belongs to a region of Europe where the British assume all responsibilities.' In its 1944 manifesto, the party insisted that its members should 'avoid taking the law into your own hands'. The party leadership backed a deal ending the first phase of the civil war on the basis of disbanding the popular resistance and the return to parliamentary politics.[146]

Social democratic and right-wing parties were the main political beneficiaries, but the communist parties played a crucial role in closing off alternative paths and ensuring politics was once more channelled through the parliamentary process in the West. This and the division of much of the world into two rival blocs, one calling itself communist, was essential to the post-war return to order.

The basis of the boom

Stabilisation would, however, have been difficult without the return of boom conditions and the post-war boom was the most sustained that capitalism had ever known. Output in the US tripled, grew five-fold in Germany and by a factor of four in France. Japan surged from relative underdevelopment to become the second biggest economy in the world. The Global South fared much worse, but the major powers were forced to give up their formal colonies and at least some parts of what became known as the Third World began to industrialise on a significant scale. Elsewhere in the South, increases in per capita income at least started to raise expectations.[147]

The boom, however, was not primarily a product of state interventions or a 'Fordist' class compromise. It was driven by a sustained level of capitalist investment, itself the result of a return to a high rate of profit beginning in the late 1930s.[148] During the decades of boom until the mid-1960s, the rate of profit averaged around twice that of the inter-war decades.[149] It wasn't until the 1960s, long after the boom had begun, that Keynesian demand management policies were adopted in full in the Western economies. As Meghnad Desai has shown: 'In the USA Keynesian policies were slow to be officially adopted… They finally triumphed with the Kennedy-Johnson tax cut of 1964.'[150] In his study of the literature, Robert Brenner found that the trajectories of the US, Japanese and German economies in this period provide 'little basis' for concluding that the extraordinary spurt of growth was attributable to the emergence of new demand through the welfare state, the 'capital-labour accord', or Keynesian demand management.[151]

Nor was any deal made in industry between workers and bosses to sustain demand. The late 1940s and 1950s were a period of bitter class struggle in which the bosses rolled out Fordist production methods and 'scientific management' across industry. In the process they clawed back the degree of shop-floor control that the unions had temporarily secured in the great struggles of the 1930s. They did their best to keep wages *down*. In the words of Aglietta, one of the champions of regulation theory, 'The entire drift of the class struggle in the United States since the war has been to transform collective bargaining into a battering ram of the employers.'[152] The result was that wage growth lagged behind productivity growth through almost the whole of the post-war boom.[153]

In so far as there were wage rises, this was a product of uncoordinated localised struggles and agreements, not some overarching economic strategy. In the words of Robert Brenner and Michael Gluck there was:

> ...never anything resembling a generalized 'social contract'... on how revenue was to be divided between investment and consumption or between profits and wages. To the degree that consumption and wages did keep up with investment and profits in consequence of developments in the private sector, it was only as an unplanned outcome of myriad uncoordinated private decisions by firms about prices and myriad employer–labour conflicts over the terms of employment.[154]

High demand for labour and relatively high profit margins drove the bosses to pay much more attention than they had in the past both to reproducing labour power and deflecting working-class discontent. The priorities were to keep the factories running and, as new technologies were developed, to ensure that there was a sufficiently trained workforce. These imperatives explain both the growth of wages such as it was and the continued expansion of welfarism through the period. All this, though, took place against the background of continued and often bitter class struggle.

What a way to make a living

How, then, did the boom affect class relations? First there was a sharp increase in the size of the working class. In the US the number of non-agricultural workers grew from 33.8 million in 1940 to 55.3 million in 1970, a rise from 65.4 per cent to 69.1 per cent of the working population.[155] In the 11 years after 1956 the non-agricultural workforce grew by nearly 12 million in Japan, 2.7 million in France and in Italy by 1.2 million in just eight years.[156]

Far from somehow increasing workers' stake in the system, boomtime investment led to a loss of control in the workplace. In his path-breaking analysis of the impact of Fordism on work lives, Harry Braverman charts how the scientific and management revolution intensified the division of labour and accelerated the deskilling of the working class. Historically, the concept of skill had been bound up with craft mastery: the combination of knowledge of materials and processes with the practiced manual dexterities required to carry on a specific branch of production. Fordism transformed the situation:

> ...the extreme concentration of this knowledge in the hands of management and its closely associated staff organizations have closed this avenue to the working population. What is left to workers is a reinterpreted and woefully inadequate concept of skill: a specific dexterity, a limited and repetitious operation, 'speed as skill,' etc. With the development of the capitalist mode of production, the very concept of skill becomes degraded along with the degradation of labour and the yardstick by which it is measured shrinks to such a point that today the worker is considered to possess a 'skill' if his or her job requires a few days' or weeks' training.[157]

This process of deskilling and loss of control affected all aspects of production. Workers in the nationalised industries found that their work lives were not transformed. They had to organise in trade unions and fight for their conditions and pay just like workers in the rest of the economy. Workers in nationalised docks, car plants and the mines turned out to be at the forefront of the new wave of struggle that emerged at the end of the long boom.

Fordism led to a massive increase in the number of white-collar workers, employed to administer and monitor the increasingly complex production and marketing processes. At the turn of the nineteenth century the proportion of clerks in the working population was 4 per cent in Great Britain and 3 per cent in the US. By 1961, 13 per cent of the working population were in white-collar occupations in Britain, and by 1970, 18 per cent in the US.[158] Workers in this 'shadow production process' had become fully proletarianized by the end of the Second World War. Wage levels were below those of blue-collar workers partly because white-collar occupations drew in large numbers of women who could be paid less. Just like factory workers, white-collar workers were subject to a degrading division of labour, and to drastic deskilling and monitoring. A US business guide to office clerical time standards from 1960 gives a flavour of the problem:[159]

Open and close	*Minutes*
File drawer, open and close, no selection	.04
Folder, open or close flaps	.04
Desk drawer, open side drawer of standard desk	.014
Open center drawer	.026
Close side	.015
Close center	.027

Chair activity	
Get up from chair	.033
Sit down in chair	.033
Tum in swivel chair	.009
Move in chair to adjoining desk or file (4 ft. maximum)	.050

When US female clerical workers began to self-organise in the early 1970s, one of their main grievances was the soul-destroying repetitiveness of their work. 'Typing pools' were paper production lines in which they complained of being 'chained to their typewriters'. For the activists of the 9 to 5 movement which inspired the famous Hollywood film of the same name, sexual harassment, unequal pay and inhuman work systems were all part of the loss of control over their lives. In the end they came to see militant workplace organising as their best hope of challenging it.[160]

Alongside the emergence of a white-collar working class, there was a sharp expansion in the sector described as 'professional or managerial'. The category includes actual managers, professionals needed to run capitalist society like planners, architects, doctors and lawyers, but also teachers and lecturers. In the 1970s, Barbara and John Ehrenreich developed an influential theory that under post-war monopoly capitalism, this group had come to form a distinct 'professional managerial class' which had interests different from both the owners of capital and workers. This class's fundamental characteristic was, according to the Ehrenreichs, that it is 'employed by capital and it manages, controls, has authority over labour'.[161]

The Ehrenreichs had identified an important development to which we shall return. Their conception of the 'professional managerial class' was however too undifferentiated. Once the various components of the category are analysed in terms of their relationship to the process of production, it becomes clear that this was not a homogenous group. On the one hand, the primary function of university principals, head teachers, top management in the civil service, local councils and hospitals, top lawyers, senior journalists and so on was to ensure the smooth running of the system. Most of them adhered to the values of the ruling class and the large salaries they received constituted a share of the capitalists' profit. However, many of the occupations grouped by the Ehrenreichs in this category actually involve very limited degrees of control over their own work process, let alone the labour of others. What is more, in the case of technicians, draughtsmen, engineers and many others, they directly contribute to the creation of surplus value. Others, like teachers and health workers, don't produce profits but do jobs that are essential to the reproduction of the working class and are therefore also essential to the creation of surplus value.

The situation was neither static nor simple. There is no doubt that in the post-war period a new kind of middle class was emerging alongside the traditional petty bourgeoisie of shop keepers, lawyers, clerks and small business people described by Marx. But it was also true that a whole range of jobs that were regarded as middle class were becoming more and more alienated and routinised. As a result, by the end of the boom not just white-collar workers but people like teachers and nurses, previously regarded as professionals, were unionising. Many of them played an important part in the industrial upturn that gathered momentum in the second half of the 1960s.

Struggle contained

The high rate of profit, the consistently high demand for labour, and the reshaping of the workforce help explain the pattern of class struggle in the period. The World Labor Group's data on labour unrest in the metropolitan countries suggest that industrial struggle remained at a relatively high level after its post-war peak with nothing like the precipitous drop of the 1920s. Strike levels began to rise in the US and many industrialised countries by the start of the 1960s.[162]

In general, however, industrial action during the boom years lost its political edge. The derailing of the post-war insurgencies, the anti-communism of the Cold War and the rollout of welfarism all encouraged this depoliticisation. But boom conditions themselves reinforced the effect, not just by creating a context in which wages could rise but also, paradoxically, by strengthening workers' bargaining position. Workers' increased leverage meant that stoppages were normally sectional and often short. In Britain, for example, the average length of strikes between 1962 and 1966 was two days.[163] In the words of one industrial relations expert, workplace bargaining became 'largely informal, largely fragmented and largely autonomous'.[164]

The impact of this was highly contradictory. A sectional and economistic working-class movement concerned mainly with narrow questions of pay and conditions allowed the space for the trade-union leaderships and the political representatives of the working class to move further to the right. This in turn reinforced political apathy amongst workers. It was, however, often accompanied by an increase in the level of plant-level organisation and a growing independence of the rank and file from the union bureaucracies in practice. As a government report into unions in Britain in the 1960s concluded, full employment had 'increased the influence of the work group' as opposed to the union officials, let alone the national union.[165] This strengthened the position of the shop steward because strikes were often over before the union full-timer showed up. British Trotskyist Tony Cliff put it like this:

> The full employment (or near full employment) of the war and the post-war period gave the workers new confidence, but at the same time fragmented the working class: sectional consciousness largely replaced class consciousness. 'Do-it-yourself' reformism was a partial advance – to self-reliance and self-activity – but also a partial retreat.[166]

The relative stability of the years of boom in the West was not then the product of changes in class structure, bourgeoisification, or a class accord or compromise. An expanding capitalism had paradoxically limited generalisation because it allowed workers relatively quick wins. This, combined with the defeat and containment of the radical movements at the end of the Second

World War and the turn towards welfarism, was enough to secure a level of social peace. The intense exploitation in the new factories and the proletarianization of whole swathes of the population was, however, storing up huge levels of discontent. Rank-and-file confidence would suddenly become a problem for the employers as the boom began to falter.

Dreams deferred

The dynamic in the developing world had similarities but also diverged. There was a higher level of struggle in the colonial and post-colonial world from the late 1940s to the early 1960s than at any other time in the century. Despite being relatively small in most colonised countries, labour movements played a vital role in many of the growing struggles for independence.[167] Strikes were central to the Quit India movement launched in 1942 which, despite being viciously repressed, convinced many of those involved in governing the colony that Britain would have to withdraw from India.[168]

A militant workers movement was central too in the cycle of struggles for full independence in Egypt that began in 1946 and ended with Abdul Nasser's successful coup in 1952. The 1947 Tanzanian general strike completely shut down the capital Dar es Salaam and was a major inspiration for the formation of the main party of independence, the Tanganyikan African National Union, in 1953.[169] A general strike in Ghana in 1949 later had a similar impact: 'The economic life of the whole country came to a standstill. All employed workers stayed home and employers, including the government, the biggest employer of all, closed down.'[170] The great African–American historian Manning Marable went as far as to argue that 'modern *nationalist* consciousness throughout much of Africa and the Caribbean was prefigured by *trade-union* consciousness and organisation.'[171]

In some places incipient forms of workers' control emerged

in the independence struggle. In Indonesia, after the defeat of both the Japanese army and Dutch troops trying to recolonise the country, workers seized control of factories, railway stations and plantations. As the new Indonesian state was still being organised, and with the country on the brink of economic breakdown, workers set up committees to organise key aspects of society, starting with the railways. One account of the rail workers' action explains how their takeover flowed directly from the independence struggle, but pointed towards a completely new way of organising their enterprises:

> Once the workers got their hands on the station operations, they began to organise in a new direction. The task of managing the railway's operation made it immediately necessary to set up an accountable, workable system of self-organisation.[172]

A similar process took place nearly two decades later in the turmoil accompanying the victory of Algerian people's struggle for independence in July 1962. In what came to be called the movement for 'Autogestion' or self-management, agricultural workers started taking over colonial estates, often because the owners had fled the country. The movement spread fast to urban areas, however, when local union organisations decided on the forced occupation of factories and commercial enterprises. As early as February 1962, the Union Generale du Travailleurs Algerian (UGTA) had called for the socialisation rather than just the nationalisation of property, arguing that: 'Independence is inseparable from the Revolution, but the Revolution is more important than independence.'[173] Many workers took them at their word, seized enterprises across the economy and set up elected committees to run them.

In both cases, however, once the post-independence regimes had consolidated themselves, they moved against workers' self-management. In Indonesia the new 'socialist' government condemned self-management as 'anarcho-syndicalist' and took measures to bring the railways and other enterprises under the control of central or local government.[174] Ben Bella's FLN government in Algeria endorsed the idea of Autogestation in its post-independence programme. It soon became clear, however, that Ben Bella had put himself at the head of the movement in order to rein it in and that he wouldn't tolerate rival centres of power. By January 1963 he had brought the UGTA under government control. His official Autogestion programme limited the areas of the economy to which self-management could apply, created an unelected national agency to administer it and placed government appointed directors in each of the enterprises.[175]

In an illuminating assessment of this process, Samuel J Southgate points out that though the radical nationalist leadership of the FLN was hostile to the existing, mainly French, bourgeoisie it was, however, based on 'technocratic and military factions of the petit bourgeoisie' and its aims were national development through an economically independent state capitalism. As result it was committed to:

> ...undermining and destroying Autogestion as created by the working class. Once self-management was formalised and the ad hoc inventions of workers disbanded, the relations of productions remained the same as far as an individual worker was concerned: the state owned the enterprise, workers received a wage, democratic participation was at a low level, and vital areas of decision making were beyond the workers' grasp.[176]

Indonesia and Algeria were outlying cases in which the struggle for independence had led to significant levels of workers' control of industry. The general approach, though, of post-colonial ruling classes to the working-class movements described here applies quite generally. As Jafar Suryomenggolo argues in a summary of case studies:

> ...most nationalist leaders in Africa and Asia, in order to serve their political purposes, were motivated to neutralise the labor movement upon capturing the political space in their newly independent states. To varying degrees, under the rhetoric of rejecting class conflict as a 'European' or 'Western' perspective, they have succeeded in subordinating the labor movement to the postcolonial state.[177]

How and why did this happen? First, from Vietnam and India to China, from Ghana and Algeria to Cuba, the independence movements were led by members of the lower middle classes: military officers, intellectuals, better-off peasants and professionals. These social groups had been excluded from power under colonial rule. Their victory, whether won through mass movements, elections or guerrilla struggle, delivered political change. Colonial elites were at least partly removed from office and the weak indigenous bourgeoisie and land-owning classes were sidelined politically. Wider sections of the economy were integrated into the state. However it came to office, the ruling party's administration tended to merge with the state apparatus. But the new rulers were hostile to the democratisation of the economy or any challenge to relations of exploitation. They were great believers in efficiency. Their aim was to drag the new nation out of stagnation through industrialisation and national capital accumulation rather than encourage a freely associated people to liberate themselves.[178]

Workers' failure to challenge for leadership of the movements partly no doubt reflected the limited social weight of the class in many of the colonial countries. This, however, is far from the whole story. Investment in mining, processing and manufacture had risen unevenly but significantly across much of the Global South from the 1920s onwards.[179] From the ports and textile mills of Egypt and India to the mines of northern Rhodesia or Trinidad, there were by the 1940s and 1950s plenty of centres of working-class power in the Global South. The early experience of revolutionary Russia in 1917 had shown how a relatively small but highly organised working class could put itself at the head of an alliance with peasants and soldiers capable of popular control of the economy and, as we have seen, working-class movements often played a strategically crucial role in galvanising the nationalist movements.

Their failure lay more in the low level of development and independence of workers' organisations. Even in the cases of Indonesia and Algeria it is clear that the emerging labour movements were fragile and lacking in independence. Samuel Southgate paints a picture of the fatally limited perspectives of the movement in Algeria, even at the point at which it had proved capable of running sections of the economy:

> Crucially, while the working class had seized control of the means of production in some of the most important sectors of the economy, it had neither set about extending workers' control on its own, nor consolidated individual units into greater organizational bodies. Thus by the fall of 1962, the process had effectively stalled and the government was in a position to assume responsibility for the movement.[180]

The situation elsewhere was similar. A study of the Indian trade-union movement at the time of independence, for example, showed that many of the unions were run by people with no background in industry and that little tradition of self-organisation had developed.[181] Another points to the connected fact that the trade-union movement at the time tended to revolve around prominent personalities rather than effective self-organisation.[182]

Once again, however, political ideas and organisation were important. Despite their hostility to working-class self-activity, let alone power, the majority of the post-colonial regimes dressed themselves up in the language of socialism. They could do this because the dominant models of socialism were Western-style social democracy, Stalinised Russia and the China of Mao Tse Tung. Countries like Ghana and Tanzania, whose independence leaders at least at first adopted a peaceful, 'democratic-socialist' strategy, explicitly ruled out the 'revolutionary romanticism' of class conflict and adopted a policy of gradualism and even co-operation with the colonial authorities. China and Russia represented forms of state capitalism in which the working class was subordinated to a new, bureaucratic ruling class.

Just as in the West the communist parties pushed for accommodation with the existing ruling classes, in the Global South they urged unity with all classes involved in the anti-colonial struggles and to limit the aspirations of the anti-colonial movements to political demands. So, for example, in Vietnam in 1946 the Communist Party-led Vietminh movement appealed to 'men and women, old and young, regardless of creeds, political parties or nationalities, all the Vietnamese must stand up to fight the French colonialists to save the fatherland'.[183] On taking power, the movement opposed land grabs by poor peasants and immediately subordinated the trade unions which became 'one of the mass organisations that carry our party policy'.[184] The same approach can be seen in Egypt. Despite being viciously repressed by the nationalist Wafd Party in the 1920s and then growing rapidly amongst workers and students in the 1930s and 1940s, the Egyptian Communist Party slavishly followed the Moscow line and worked in alliance with the Wafd during the post-war independence struggles.

As a result, the greatest hopes raised by national liberation were dashed. Living standards improved in many places and varying degrees of progress were made in education and welfare, but whatever the rhetoric, the basic strategy was to develop a state-led national capitalism. What the Working People's Alliance of Guyana called 'a bourgeoisie of a new type' tended to emerge, their control of the new state giving them the base 'from which they seize the social surplus to divert it not only to personal consumption, but to private accumulation with the aim of building indigenous capitalism'.[185] In a few cases, state-driven development led to significant economic growth, turning former colonies like Brazil, Singapore and South Korea into major players in the world market. Elsewhere, unequal terms of trade blocked progress and even sometimes brutal levels of exploitation couldn't generate adequate funds for investment. Many countries in the South ended up falling victim to the debt trap of the 1980s and were forced to open up their economies to the world market, with disastrous results.

The unexpected upsurge

The slowing of the boom was accompanied by an explosion of social protest. There have been many attempts to cast the revolt of 1968 and the following years as a mainly student phenomenon driven by a clash of generation or lifestyle. In these accounts, dropping out, dropping acid and exploring sexuality morphed easily into a celebration of individuality and even consumerism. Here 1968 has no prehistory beyond the growth of mass production and the emergence of youth culture. Such interpretations completely fail to explain 1968's seismic shock. The protests that erupted that year certainly threw every aspect of society and behaviour into question. They sparked a new wave of feminist activism and gave rise to the gay liberation movement. They also quickly threatened governments and led to a global cycle of militant struggle which at moments rocked the foundations of the capitalist system itself. Far from being simply student or youth protests, at their most challenging, they had working-class organisation at their heart. 1968 was a product of fundamental contradictions that had been building up in the system over the years of the long boom.

Three key events of the year, the assassination of Martin Luther King, the Vietnamese Tet offensive against the US occupation of Vietnam, and the May general strike in France neatly indicate the fault lines. The civil-rights struggle against the structural racism in the US South had been one of the few focuses of opposition to the status quo in the US in the 1950s and early 1960s, and many leading figures of 1968 were involved in it. By the mid-1960s, however, the movement was in a crisis caused by its failure to challenge the racism embedded in the Democratic Party and more importantly, in the northern cities to which millions of black people from the South had emigrated during the boom years. The result of this was the radicalisation of the movement and a series of riots in major US cities that in some cases had the scale and tenacity of urban uprisings. Such open insurgency in the heartlands of US capitalism sent shock waves around the world.

Accompanying this was a radicalising student movement. Higher education had expanded massively during the boom years to produce enough managers, technicians, teachers and other skilled workers to staff modernising industries and fast-growing state bureaucracies. In Britain, for example, there were 69,000 students in Britain at the start of the Second World War. By 1972 the number had risen almost tenfold to 600,000, 15 per cent of the age group.[186] The explosions of 1968 were foreshadowed by waves of student protests and sit-ins from Berkeley, California in 1964 and the Free University of West Berlin in 1966, to the London School of Economics and many German and Italian universities in 1967. The students expressed outrage at what they saw as the industrialisation of education and a growing disconnect between liberal ideology and the reality on the ground.[187] By 1970, radical ideas had mainstreamed amongst students, with one national US poll finding that 75 per cent of students believed 'basic changes to the system' were needed in the US.[188]

The main catalyst was the Vietnam War. It was the Students for a Democratic Society that called the first major national demonstration in Washington against the Vietnam War in 1965.[189] As the war escalated and the draft widened, the movement grew exponentially at home and started to internationalise. In April 1967, 400,000 people assembled for an anti-war demonstration in New York. In June 1967, police in Berlin raised the profile and the temperature of the movement by viciously attacking a protest against visiting US Vice President Hubert Humphrey. In 1968 itself, German students hosted a 4000-strong international anti-war conference, 100,000 marched against the war in London, and sentiment over Vietnam helped detonate the French student riots. Tellingly, too, striking Fiat workers in northern Italy remapped the anti-colonial struggle onto their own industrial conflict and declared that 'Vietnam is in our factories'.[190]

Intersecting with this political radicalisation were the accumulated stresses on the working class generated by the boom. In the countries where industry had drawn in new workforces fastest and imposed new working practices most brutally, discontent had led to spontaneous outbreaks of militancy from the early 1960s. In his novel of factory revolt, *We Want Everything*, the Italian militant Nanni Balestrini gives a sense of the shock of dehumanisation felt by young people, often from the South, entering the factories for the first time:

On the Fiat line it's not a question of learning but of getting your muscles used to it, of getting used to the force of those movements and the rhythm. Having to place a whatchamacallit every twenty seconds meant you had movements quicker than a heartbeat. That is a finger, your eye, any part was forced to move in tenths of a second: forced actions in fractions of a second. The action of choosing the two washers, the action of choosing the two bolts, those movements were actions your muscles and your eyes had to make by themselves, without you deciding anything. I just had to keep up the rhythm of all those movements, repeated in order and equally. Without three or four days to get used to the rhythm, you just couldn't do it.[191]

The boom years had generated some combination of working-class dissatisfaction and increased combativity almost everywhere. The number of strikes in Britain outside of the mines trebled between the mid-1950s and the mid-1960s, the vast majority of them unofficial.[192] In Japan, significant sections of workers had taken action alongside students in the movement that brought down the Kishi government in 1960. In France in 1965, a series of rotating strikes were met with lockouts, police attacks on strikers and the mass sacking of militants. Further clashes between strikers and the CRS riot police took place in 1967 in a number of key factories.[193] It was in France, of course, that the various different pressures first fused explosively in 1968. President De Gaulle, who had come to power in 1958 to head off a military coup in Algeria, led a deeply authoritarian government focussed on forcing up the competitiveness of French industry. The result was an expanding industrial workforce under fierce attack by employers and the state, and a massive student population crammed into woefully unsuitable university spaces.

The French student movement was sparked amongst other things by protests against single sex dormitories, but it quickly channelled all the frustrations of the student body into dramatic and sustained confrontations with the police on Paris's Left Bank. Initially the leaders of the union and the Communist Party denounced the student protestors as 'false revolutionaries' and 'the sons of rich bourgeois', but spontaneous solidarity from ordinary workers forced a change of line. Workers' sympathy with the students escalated into a country-wide wave of factory occupations which brought France to a halt in what remains the longest general strike in history.

The French May was the first of a cycle of working-class revolts across Europe and beyond. In Italy, two red years of factory agitation and occupation from 1969 to 1970 led to the creation of new workers' committees right across the northern industrial belt and the spectacular growth of the revolutionary left. A wave of working-class militancy accompanied the formation of the socialist Popular Unity government of Allende in Chile in 1970, which was then brutally crushed by the Pinochet coup in 1973. Insurgent strikes rocked the military regime in East and West Pakistan at the end of 1968. In Britain, Labour's attempts to implement a new incomes policy 'in place of strife' helped spark a wave of strikes, a 'wage explosion', which was led by traditionally militant groups like engineers and car workers but was joined for the first time by teachers, other public-sector workers and traditionally unorganised factory workers.[194] In Portugal, a revolution which began in 1974 as a protest against the fascist Caetano's continued colonialism ended up toppling his regime.

These upheavals were more profound than is often admitted. One indication of the level of crisis generated by the French general strike was the episode of 29 May when President De Gaulle went missing without explanation. It turned out he had fled to Baden-Baden in West Germany, apparently in despair. According to some accounts, one of his generals had to beg him to stay the course. The mass workers' struggles that began in 1969 in Italy slipped out of the control of the union leaders and created a deep 'crisis of the institutions' that lasted until well into the second half of the 1970s. The Portuguese revolution not only brought down the fascist regime but led to an alliance between workers and sections of the army which brought into question the continued existence of the Portuguese state.[195]

These are histories which repay close attention from the point of view of strategy and tactics. But a few general points are important. First, despite its antecedents, the upsurge was a complete surprise to many on the left, who had come to believe that workers were depoliticised and incorporated into capitalism and that the system could absorb 'merely' economic demands. Just months before May 1968, French socialist writer André Gorz wrote that the left's best hope was pushing for reforms because there was no chance that partial economic demands could generalise into an anti-systemic movement:

> The working class will neither unite politically, nor man the barricades, for a 10 per cent rise in wages or 50,000 more council flats. In the foreseeable future there will be no crisis of European capitalism so dramatic as to drive the mass of workers to revolutionary general strikes or armed insurrection in defence of their vital interests.[196]

The events of 1968 exploded this kind of economistic thinking. They showed that class struggle can take sudden leaps even when there is no 'dramatic' economic crisis and when the left is unresponsive. Those sceptical of workers' capacity to resist were missing the fact that in periods of growth in the productive forces, workers acquire new needs, and that the gap between their needs and the available purchasing power grows wider. Even in relatively favourable conditions for capital accumulation overall, fear of losing out internationally also still forces governments to move against workers in ways that can lead to generalisation. Especially at moments of wider questioning in society, the connections between politics and economics then suddenly become clear.

In 1968, the accumulated confidence that had been built out of economic struggles and the political apathy that accompanied them took on a new aspect. Workers had been organising effectively without much support from union leaderships. Their grievances had largely been ignored by social-democratic parties. The result was that their alienation could flip over into revolt:

> The concept of apathy or privatisation is not a static concept. At a certain stage of development – when the path of individual reforms is being narrowed, or closed – apathy can transform into its opposite, swift mass action. However, this new turn comes as an outgrowth of a previous stage; the epilogue and the prologue combine. Workers who have lost their loyalty to the traditional organisations, which have shown themselves to be paralysed over the years, are forced into extreme, explosive struggles on their own.[197]

Secondly, the history of 1968 and beyond points once again to the tremendous impact of working-class insurgencies. It shows that workers in developed capitalist societies have an enormous social weight in struggle because of their unique ability to disrupt the flow of profits and the day-to-day functioning of society. Sustained strikes created a social crisis in France, Italy and Portugal, throwing the ruling class in each country onto the defensive and raising questions about the survival of the status quo. It confirmed that once class struggle reaches this kind of intensity, it raises fundamental questions of democracy and control. Factory occupations and various forms of elected strike committees emerged directly from the needs of the struggle, involved wide layers of the workforce and generated intense discussion about how industry and wider society should be organised. During the French strike, for example, there were cases of managers being removed, factories being converted to make 'useful goods' and strike committees reaching out to establish direct relations of exchange with farmers.[198]

Such subversion at the heart of the economy tends to be infectious and to inspire groups way beyond the core of the organised working class. Immigrant communities saw the French general strike as an opportunity to challenge structural injustices. At the end of May, the 'Action Committee of Workers and Students from Countries Under French Colonial Domination' occupied a government immigration centre, accusing the government of running 'a new slave trade'.[199] Teachers and school students started to question the centralised and conservative curriculum. There was a heated debate in the medical profession and calls for an end to traditional hierarchies in medical schools and hospitals. Even footballers occupied the headquarters of the French Football Federation, locking up the general secretary and raising the red flag and the slogan 'Football for the footballers'.[200] This deep democratisation is tremendously isolating for the ruling groups. It also clearly points forward to different ways of organising things.

If the occupations, the strike committees and the inter-factory co-ordinations of these years hinted at new ways of organising society, it is also true that they quickly disappeared as the struggles subsided. The flip side of the unexpected, explosive nature of the events of these years was that they dissipated before most of the activists had time to grasp the full significance of their own actions. The struggles of these years revealed once again that because it is challenging such an all-pervasive system, to be victorious, working-class struggle for system change requires a high level of consciousness, and such consciousness cannot develop fully in the heat of relatively short bursts of struggle.

Once again, events had raised the need for specifically revolutionary organisation within the class. Without it, even the most radical movements can ultimately be contained. With the exception of Chile, the great working-class insurgencies of 1968 and after were essentially absorbed rather than repressed.

At a certain point, the movements had to confront the question of state power or accept a return to business as usual on rather better terms. The relatively small revolutionary organisations were ultimately overwhelmed by the trade-union leaderships and political forces, including the communist parties, working for a return to normality and to parliament as the locus of politics. The result was that reformism reasserted itself and reintegrated the working class into the process of capital accumulation. This was just at the time when the boom was ending and the ruling class was considering a new assault.

5. Going Underground

The dream of the 1970s New Right was to inflict decisive defeats on the working class and to bury the idea of class altogether. This involved them in the delicate project of waging ruthless class war while insisting that class no longer existed. The result is the current disorientating situation in which working people continue to suffer sustained attack while the very existence of the working class is questioned.

Neoliberal ascendancy was far from guaranteed. The struggles of the late 1960s and early 1970s had led to high levels of working-class organisation and had brought class back into the discussion. They had even forced social-democratic parties to brush off their class rhetoric.[201] The success of what came to be called the neoliberal experiment depended first on the failure of those same social-democratic parties actually to defend workers during the crises of the 1970s; second on decisive ruling-class victories against workers in a series of set-piece struggles; and thirdly on widespread acceptance of the inevitability of the changes they sought.

The neoliberal battle plan was developed by the New Right in the US and Britain to deal with crisis and restore profit levels. It was presented as a value-free technical economic fix. Like any project to restore profits, however, it had the transfer of wealth and power from workers to capitalists at its heart. In their more candid moments, the New Right were clear about what they were doing. In the words of one of their British champions at the time, 'Old fashioned Tories say there isn't any class war. New Tories make no bones about it: we are class warriors and we expect to be victorious.'[202]

Publicly, however, the New Right tried to remove class from the discussion. In the UK, Alfred Sherman, a key adviser to the Tories' new leader Margaret Thatcher, gave a series of lectures aimed at proving that class was a 'Marxist term which has no meaning in any non-Marxist schema'.[203] Thatcher echoed this later with her claim that 'class was a communist concept'.[204] Keith Joseph, one of Thatcher's closest confidantes, saw the aim of their project as creating a society in which it would be possible to claim 'we are all bourgeois now'.[205] The US New Right's ideas were influentially trailed in Kevin Phillips book *The Emerging Republican Majority*, which proposed using racism and 'status resentment' to realign white northern workers and southern rednecks around a neo-populist Republican leadership. For Phillips, the aim was to build 'a cultural siege engine out of the populist steel of Idaho, Mississippi and working-class Milwaukee, and then blast the Eastern liberal establishment to ideological smithereens'.[206]

In the beginning was the deed

The failure of the post-war Keynesian 'settlement' and the disastrous response from the Labour government in Britain, the Democrats in the USA and social democrats elsewhere provided the conditions for the rise of the right.[207] Their surrender helped create the context in which Thatcher and Reagan could gain office in 1979 and 1981 respectively. Though these election results were vital victories for the right, however, they were not the end game. In late 1981, after eighteen months in office, Thatcher was the most unpopular prime minister in British history, with approval ratings of just 25 per cent. Reagan was elected in 1980 on the lowest voter turnout for more than 30 years. Polls showed that his victory was the result of confusion and disorientation rather than a decisive hardening to the right.[208] It was key battles with organised workers that secured the right's aims and gave neoliberalism viability.

Soon after being elected, Reagan launched what was later proved to be a long-planned war against the public-sector unions. When nearly 13,000 air traffic controllers in the PATCO union went on strike in a dispute about new contracts, Reagan fired them all and insisted they would never get their jobs back. A huge scabbing operation was organised to keep planes flying. Despite warnings about travel chaos and accidents, within days 80 per cent of flights were operating normally. The union conceded defeat and the administration punished them ruthlessly, imposing a lifetime ban on rehiring the strikers and ensuring that the PATCO union was derecognised.

Reagan's aggression sent a clear message. In the words of the director of the Office of Personnel Management at the time: 'When the president said no...American business leaders were given a lesson in managerial leadership that they could not and did not ignore.'[209] Bosses across the country launched anti-union offensives, sacking union members and rehiring non-union labour. The number of recorded strike days fell from around 750,000 per year to 250,000 by the end of the decade.[210]

Years before Thatcher's election the Tories had also drawn up an action plan to take on the unions. Known as the Ridley Plan, the document advised taking on the organised working-class section by section, starting with the weakest and moving on to the key sectors, in particular the miners. The secret plan recommended forming large mobile police units capable of breaking up mass pickets like those that had closed down the coke plant at Saltley Gates. It also suggested the stockpiling of coal, ensuring that some key ports could be kept open and persuading haulage companies to build up teams of non-union drivers who would be prepared to cross picket lines with police protection.[211]

Thatcher and her cabinet implemented this plan almost to the letter and with great effect. Soon after she was elected, Thatcher took on the unions in British Steel and won. In 1983, an initial assault on the printers' unions successfully trialled new police tactics and kit for use against mass pickets.[212] By 1984, Thatcher was ready to take on the miners, the most powerful section of

British workers. All the elements of the Ridley Plan were in place including squads of semi-militarised police trained to attack and intimidate picketing miners. After a heroic 11-month struggle in which they received active support from across the working class, the miners were beaten.

The defeat was far from inevitable. Secret papers show that at least twice during the dispute Thatcher considered resigning.[213] The miners' defeat was a devastating blow to the labour movement and a green light to employers to go onto the offensive across industry. From the moment of that defeat the number of strike days went into free fall and haven't recovered since.[214] The defeat of the strike caused enough demoralisation amongst working people to secure Thatcher's third election victory in 1987 and the full rollout of her privatisation agenda.

There were similar, decisive attacks on workers in other countries in the 1970s and 1980s. General Pinochet's 1973 coup which crushed Chile's experiment with parliamentary socialism famously enabled an early and particularly brutal experiment in monetarist economics. In India, a long ruling-class assault on workers was bookended by the smashing of the railway workers in 1974 and the humiliation of the millworkers of Bombay, Calcutta and Ahmedabad in 1983.[215] In Italy a showdown with Fiat workers in 1980 ended in a terrible defeat for the unions, leading to a generalised employers' offensive and a concerted government campaign of cuts and deflation.

Levels of industrial action were falling across most of the core capitalist countries by the early 1980s, leading to crisis in their respective labour movements.[216] Everywhere the offensive paved the way for decades of restructuring, lay-offs and attacks on wages and security, and led to mushrooming unemployment and weakened labour movements. In parts of the Global South, the attacks, driven partly by the International Monetary Fund's 'structural adjustment' programmes, came a little later. The slump in strike figures here started later too, but was as precipitous as that in the north.[217] An ILO study of strikes in 38 nations showed that strike activity had fallen by 80 per cent from the 1970s to the early 2000s.[218]

Going with the flow

These ruling-class victories cleared the way for a whole new management ideology, welcoming the end of collectivism. A welter of new books appeared celebrating downsizing, outsourcing and temping. The idea of the end of the permanent working class became all the rage on both sides of the Atlantic. Irish business guru Charles Handy could claim in 1994: 'Before very long, having a proper job inside an organisation will be a minority occupation.'[219]

Such ideas were only encouraged by the continuing collapse of social democracy in the face of the neoliberal offensive. Germany's social-democratic chancellor, Helmut Schmidt, had made his peace with profit-making in 1976, arguing: 'The profits of enterprises today are the investments of tomorrow, and the investments of tomorrow are the employment of the day after.'[220] French socialist leader Francois Mitterrand came to office in 1981 on a radical manifesto committed to bucking the markets, but collapsed under pressure and implemented a round of vicious austerity measures starting in 1983. In Britain, Labour's new leader, Neil Kinnock, refused to back the miners during their great strike and spent the rest of the 1980s attacking the left in Labour and pulling the party away even from traditional social-democratic policies of renationalisation and trade-union rights. 'Them and us are gone now,' he insisted, 'we are all in it together.'[221]

As neoliberal dogma hardened in the later 1980s and early 1990s, even minimal state intervention came into question.[222] Blair's Labour Party discarded all fiscal policy activism in favour of rule-based austerity, handing over the levers of monetary policy to unelected central bankers, continuing the deregulation of the financial markets and unconditionally supporting financial globalisation. Crucially, Blair's 'New Labour' presented pro-market policies in the language of meritocracy, equal opportunity and even social justice. Blair called his Labour Party 'a broad-based movement for progress and justice', out to build a country 'where merit comes before privilege, run for the many not the few'.[223] His modernising, equal-rights image was enhanced by the introduction of legislation making real gains for LGBT people, including civil partnerships, the right to adopt and the equalisation of the age of consent.

Social democrats' love-in with free markets was accompanied by a retreat from class by a host of left intellectuals. French socialist André Gorz led the way with his 1982 book *Farewell to the Working Class*, arguing that the new economy had eroded the basis of traditional class solidarities.[224] Variations on the theme were presented by a string of left intellectuals, from the Argentinian Ernest Laclau and his Belgian partner Chantal Mouffe to the British proponents of the theory of New Times, Stuart Hall and Charles Leadbetter. After the defeats of the 1970s and early 1980s and in the new 'post-Fordist' economy that followed, the working class was apparently no longer capable of or interested in resistance to exploitation.[225] Even more 'orthodox' Marxists began to express unease at an understanding of society based on the central fact of exploitation. Eric Olin Wright and Richard D Wolff were amongst the self-proclaimed Marxists convinced that it was time to jettison Marx's idea that the 'labour-capital contradiction' was the primary contradiction in society.[226]

In the neoliberal gloom that followed, left-leaning writers suggested all sorts of new concepts of society without a working class at its centre. Italian autonomists Hardt and Negri replaced the idea with a loosely defined multitude whose boundless creativity has somehow been captured by an ill-defined relation of 'Empire'.[227] More prosaically, British academic Guy Standing won widespread support for his view that the working class had been replaced by a new series of classes. These included the 'salariat', highly-paid and highly-skilled 'proficians'; a dwindling core of manual workers; and the 'precariat', a rapidly growing sector suffering from chronic and structural insecurity with different interests and concerns from the narrowing groups of permanent workers.[228] Standing helped clear the way to the notion of workers as a privileged layer exemplified in Slavoj Zizek's comment: 'Who dares strike today, when having a permanent job is itself a privilege? Not low-paid workers in (what remains of) the textile industry, etc., but those privileged workers who have guaranteed jobs.'[229]

Meanwhile, theorists of 'the new capitalism' claimed that labour, in so far as it exists, nowadays produces immaterial goods like information, knowledge, images and relationships rather than tangible or quantifiable things. The service sector, a massive category which includes rail transport, road haulage, refuse collection, cleaning and IT amongst much else, was widely assumed to be completely separate from the world of production and commodities. Influential sociologist Manuel Castells brought many of these ideas together in a series of studies which painted a picture of a networked society focussed on communication and an immaterial knowledge economy whose 'flows' cannot be pinned down to concepts of commodity, exploitation or surplus value. In his 2010 work *The Power of Identity*, Manuel Castells drew the conclusion that now has common currency; that all these processes render socialism hopelessly outdated and leave us only with a multitude of identity-based resistances.[230]

Actually existing capitalism

Any serious analysis of recent production trends, class relations and patterns of struggle shows that the various attempts to downplay class were and are completely misleading. Neoliberalism has, of course, drastically re-ordered production and traumatically reshaped the working class internationally. In both the older capitalist economies and the developing world, whole industries have been destroyed, new technologies have sprung up, production has been relocated and state support for workers and the poor has been slashed.

At the same time, however, there has been a sharp *growth* in the size of the global working class. For the first time in history, wage-earning is now the majority experience globally.[231] Kim Moody estimates in his 2018 study of the US working class that the global wage-earning non-agricultural workforce grew from 1.5 billion in 1999 to 2.1 billion in 2013, making it about half of the world's workforce. At the same time, he estimates that, despite the recession, the number of industrial workers rose from 533.2 million in 1999 to 724.2 million in 2013, with a dramatic shift towards developing countries.[232]

In the core capitalist countries, there has been breakneck technological innovation, some de-industrialisation, a big expansion in the so-called service sector, an explosion of outsourcing and the associated privatisation of swathes of the public sector. All of this is part of a sustained employers' offensive on many fronts, leading to wage cuts, de-unionisation and the introduction of new, inhuman, lean and high surveillance management methods. The result has been a sharp decline in working-class living standards as well as a record low level of industrial resistance. This has all been traumatic for working people. But it has not produced a world of immaterial labour, a frictionless economy, the end of the working class or all-pervading precarity.

The number of industrial workers in the developed economies fell from 122 million in 1999 to 107 million in 2013. The US alone lost 5.7 million manufacturing jobs between 1979 and 2010.[233] The UK has been amongst the worst affected, as manufacturing employment here has halved since 1978.[234] This is still, however, an awfully long way from terminal de-industrialisation. The US still employs more than 12 million manufacturing workers and the figure has been rising recently.[235] In Germany, more than a quarter of workers still work in industry. In terms of actual output as opposed to employment, manufacturing remains a crucial, often growing sector of all developed economies. The fact is, in the US, manufacturing output has been rising for years. As *The Economist* magazine pointed out, 'for all the bellyaching about the "decline of American manufacturing" and "the shifting of production en masse to China", real output has been growing at an annual pace of almost 4 per cent since 1991, faster than GDP growth'.[236]

What this shows is that while neoliberal globalisation has massively boosted the communication and transport sectors, it hasn't generated anything approximating an 'immaterial' or 'circulation' economy. The mushrooming of services and what has been called a 'logistics revolution' have in fact taken place in the context of an *increase* in the production of physical commodities globally and in the old capitalist economies. It suggests too that the bulk of capitalist accumulation still takes place through standard forms of work-based exploitation, rather than through land grabbing and the ransacking of the public sphere or commons, 'accumulation through dispossession', as David Harvey describes it. These are real processes which have had devastating effects. But as Raju Das argues, the increase in productivity and the number of workers internationally renders claims that these types of accumulation are the defining characteristics of neoliberal capitalism implausible.

It also underlines that, although there has been a sharp proportionate shift in industrial production to the Global South, neoliberal restructuring has not involved a simple transfer of manufacturing from the developed to the less developed world. The extent of offshoring to the Global South has in fact been deliberately exaggerated to undermine workers' confidence in the core. In most Western countries, the overwhelming majority of job losses can be put down to increased productivity rather than offshoring. It is the result of the introduction of lean production methods, new technology, and the general counter-offensive against labour; in other words, the class struggle itself. There is, in fact, more and more evidence of jobs in some sectors coming back to core countries, as the process of creating new centres of accumulation abroad has generated working-class resistance and increased labour costs.[237]

The distinction between services and manufacturing is in any case often quite arbitrary and certainly can't be seen as differentiating between productive and non-productive or non-profitable parts of the economy. The reality is that many 'service-sector' jobs in fact involve the physical transformation of inputs into increased value outputs. Jobs in, for example, food services, cleaning, transport, hotels, hospitals, maintenance and entertainment are mainly in the private sector, organised along capitalist lines and producing some sort of commodity. A huge proportion of these jobs are low-skilled and low-paid. Very few are recognisably white-collar, let alone 'immaterial'. Most of them are routine, many are manual and they often require little training. Even where the product is data, research or other forms of knowledge, output is calculated, rationalised and commodified. As one study of the IT workforce points out, 'Work of expert or scientific labour is subject to exploitation and control... for example, through performance metrics, project monitoring procedures, packaged software products and automation.'[238] The knowledge produced doesn't remain the property of the worker but is separated from them like any other commodity.

Because more and more service industries are run by private capital and because their work processes are so similar to those in manufacturing, they are subject to the same kind of monitoring and lean production regimes that we have seen in factories and offices in the last few decades. They are also often very tightly physically attached to particular locations and not open to being 'offshored'.[239] Even where services remain in the public sector, they constitute a social cost to the capitalists that they have to fund partly out of their profits. The neoliberal state is constantly looking for ways to marketize them if they can, and get away with the absolute minimum provision possible if they can't. Consequently, the neoliberal years have been marked by the introduction of internal markets, incentives and heavy surveillance into the public sector, often making the work experience there virtually indistinguishable from the private.

One indication that neoliberalism has transformed the working class, rather than terminally fragmenting it, is that workplace size has held fairly steady over the last four decades. In Britain, the number of workers in workplaces of more than one thousand has fallen a little, but the total working in enterprises of more than 500 appears to have gone up.[240] In the US, the numbers in workplaces of over 1000 went up from 10.7 million, or 13 per cent of the workforce, in 1986, to 16.5 million, or 14 per cent of the workforce, in 2008.[241] There are still plenty of large manufacturing or mining plants, but their overall number has fallen, while what are called service-sector workplaces have sharply increased in average size. This has been driven by the growth in the health, warehousing, transport and finance sectors, but even sales workers are now mainly concentrated in big-box retail outlets, supermarkets and call centres.

Neoliberalism has created an epidemic of workplace insecurity. One recent international survey found that '83 percent of employees say they fear losing their job, attributing it to the gig economy, a looming recession, a lack of skills, cheaper foreign competitors, immigrants who will work for less, automation, or jobs being moved to other countries.'[242] Waves of job cuts and unemployment, most notably in the 1980s and after the 2008 recession, created a climate of fear. As Charles Umney argues, because financialised capitalism tends to be concerned more about shareholder value than long-term profitability, its watchwords are 'downsize and distribute' rather than 'retain and reinvest'.[243]

The result is that workers are often in permanent fear of changes in work practices, outsourcing, pay cuts, closures or lay-offs. The sense of insecurity is also partly a product of the gulf between young people's aspirations and the economic system's capacity to meet them. Growing numbers of young people describe themselves as trapped in what they regard as temporary low-paid jobs and feeling as if there is no way out.[244] Meanwhile, households have become more and more caught up in a financial system that promotes private debt and retail services such as credit cards, mortgages and student loans, all of which increase anxiety in the present and uncertainty about the future.[245]

Insecurity is also generated directly by new forms of super-exploitative work relationships. Zero-hours contracts and the gig economy in general have used the internet to replicate forms of extreme casualisation most hoped had died out a century ago. Both the hospitality and, shockingly, the social-care sector are dominated by these kinds of extreme precarity. Despite this, neoliberalism has not generated an economy dominated by formally precarious work as Guy Standing and many others claim. In Britain, 90 per cent of the workforce remain in directly employed, formally permanent jobs. Things appear quite similar in the US, where around 85 per cent of those in work are in permanent jobs. When surveyed, the number of people in the US who said they had been in the same job for ten years or more fell by 5 per cent from 1973 to 2006, and then rose again across the age range from 2006 to 2016.[246]

Pressure points

The reality is that the working class in the West has not been terminally atomised, shrunk, exported or otherwise made marginal to the economy. What has happened is that it has been reorganised as part of a massive restructuring of the production process. Once we accept that neoliberalism was always about intensifying exploitation, not bypassing it, this is hardly surprising. The expansion of manufacturing and the global growth of the working class show that on the world scale the central relation of exploitation has become more, not less, important. The restructuring that has resulted has been combined with assaults on the trade unions, as it has been driven partly by the need to break up centres of militancy and fragment patterns of collective bargaining. It has turned many people's experience of work into a nightmare and massively weakened working-class organisation. As in previous such restructurings, however, new concentrations of labour and potential centres of working-class leverage and power are emerging.

If the initial impact of the neoliberal offensive in the 1980s was one of decentralising production and outsourcing, particularly in the so-called service sector, the expansion of capital accumulation has centralised capital once again and reorganised the production of goods and services across large spaces. This has all sorts of implications. One of the ways in which outsourcing initially undermined union organising and representation was that it broke up bargaining relationships and created a situation where would-be union organisers sometimes didn't even know who to negotiate with. Now, the service sector is dominated by a handful of often global companies with profiles to match. Unionisation campaigns at the likes of Amazon, Serco and Starbucks are becoming co-ordinated and are now themselves gaining visibility.

Far from being a sign of the disappearance of the working class, the expansion of the service sector has created new potential focusses of resistance. For one thing, the spiralling number of service workers employed to maintain corporate capital and states' fixed assets in fact have tremendous leverage in one of Western capitalism's growth areas: the provision of production services, particularly for the financial sector. Cleaners, caterers, security staff and maintenance workers in corporate office buildings, call centres, government buildings, as well as universities and hospitals, are essential to the accumulation of profits, or at least the daily functioning of key institutions. This is a fact recognised in their designation as 'key workers' during the pandemic. Strikes in this sector have immediate and damaging impact.

These workers normally operate in workplaces that are largely immovable and are not therefore vulnerable to a spatial fix. A Western corporation cannot send its headquarters to a country in the Global South to be cleaned every night. Moreover, the investment in telecommunication networks and wiring systems necessary for buildings with advanced communications capabilities make permanently moving the command-and-control centres of modern capitalism extremely costly.[247] It is not surprising then that some important victories have been won by workers organising and taking action in these sectors in the last few decades.[248]

The logistics revolution has created enormous vulnerabilities for capital. The new economy may not be quite as thoroughly globalised as some of its boosters suggest, but commodities of all kinds circulate the globe to an unprecedented degree. Such mobility relies on an enormous, immobile, material infrastructure, networks of industry, logistics, communications and commerce. As Kim Moody argues in *On New Terrain*, whatever some commentators may say, logistics workers who help link the production chain and bring goods to the market are part of the process of production, 'The supply chain, from raw materials to the very doors of Wal-Mart is, in the Marxist view, a production assembly line.'[249]

The source of logistics workers' bargaining power is to be found not just in the direct impact of their actions on their immediate employers, but also on the upstream/downstream impact of the failure to deliver goods, services and people to their destination. Once again, few spatial fixes are available to the employers. Particularly troublesome nodes might be taken out of a distribution network in extreme cases, but the impact is likely to be heavy for all the connected industries. What is more, as David Harvey has pointed out, 'Roads, railways, canals, airports, etc., cannot be moved without the value embodied in them being lost.'[250]

A paradox that escapes the prophets of ultra-mobile capital is that both communication systems and the mobility of its goods require massive investment in fundamentally immobile capital.

As Kim Moody points out, however, the tendency of competition to generate more concentration and centralisation in the era of globalisation can create more serious headaches for capital. It has in fact meant that some of the problems restructuring was designed to overcome have re-emerged, and at a higher level. As Moody says, 'More and more aspects of production are tied together in just-in-time supply chains that have reproduced the vulnerability that capital sought to escape through lean production methods and relocation.'[251] Just-in-time production chains give workers in transport, warehousing and associated communications even more power. Many of these logistics workers tend to be concentrated too in huge distribution hubs around seaports, intermodal yards or 'metropolises', which are normally situated in or near major cities:

Millions of service, sales, and even office workers now work in larger, more capital-intensive workplaces. They are increasingly linked together in vulnerable technology-driven supply chains, themselves organized around enormous logistics clusters that concentrate tens and even hundreds of thousands of workers in finite geographical sites.[252]

It doesn't take much imagination to realise that these

concentrations of workers strategically placed around the globe at the heart of enormous, interconnected, just-in-time supply chains have tremendous potential to disrupt the accumulation of capital in short order.

Education is another pressure point in the global production process. While we don't live in the free-flowing knowledge economy of some commentators' fantasies, data and information processing have become increasingly important elements of the production process, and consequently teachers at all levels have become absolutely integral to the new economy. The number of teachers worldwide began to rise sharply in the second half of last century, growing from 8 million in 1950 to 47 million in 1990. By 2014 there were an estimated 83 million teachers around the world.[253] Teachers, of course, have not had any control over their means of production for a long time. They have to sell their labour to an employer, still normally the state. They are highly skilled workers and therefore relatively difficult to replace at short notice, but as their importance in producing new generations of workers has increased, they have had less and less control over their curriculum and have faced a more and more bureaucratised labour process. This contradiction between their social role in developing other human beings and an increasingly unmanageable and 'industrial' work process has created immense dissatisfaction.

It is not just their skill level that gives teachers power. So far, there has been little technological innovation in schools. This means that an expansion of the educational system leads directly to the expanding employment of teachers, rather than the introduction of labour-saving technologies and potential bouts of unemployment. Also, teachers are strategically and uniquely embedded in the social division of labour. As Beverly Silver argues:

Teachers' strikes have ripple effects throughout the social

division of labor – disrupting family routines and making it difficult for working parents to do their own jobs. Moreover, where there have been exceptionally long and/or frequent strikes in education (or widespread teacher hostility toward their employers), fears have been raised about the longer-term impact of teacher labor unrest on the final product – that is, students' educational accomplishments as well as their proper socialization as citizens.[254]

Education was one of the few sectors that has seen a rising trend of labour unrest over the last few decades.[255] Teachers' strikes have been a central feature of resistance to cuts and austerity across the developed and underdeveloped world. It was mainly teachers' strikes that made 2018 the biggest year for workers' protests in the US in a generation. They were also a feature of labour unrest in dozens of countries across five continents in 2019.[256]

Neoliberalism has also had a profound effect on the makeup of the working class. Until recently at least, the expansion of the service sector has boosted the number of women in the workforce. In the US, women's participation in the labour market has nearly doubled since 1950, from 34 per cent of working-age women to almost 57 per cent in 2016. The UK has seen an almost continual rise in the proportion of women in employment up from 57 per cent in 1975 to a record high of 78 per cent in 2017.[257] Sixty per cent of essential workers are women in the UK. The proportion of women working has gone up across the core countries and beyond but everywhere it has been combined with a massive gender pay gap.[258]

At the same time, women continue to do the vast bulk of unpaid labour at home and state support for families has been slashed. The result is that the great gain for millions of women around the world of entry to the workforce has been won at the cost of enormous extra pressure and stress. One of the results has been a new wave of women's activism focussed partly on the pay gap and partly on sexual violence and harassment so prevalent in workplaces and across many of the institutions of capitalist society.

The 'new economy', its accompanying wars, record migration flows and incarcerations have created new and recharged existing forms of racism. As a number of studies have shown, capitalists have leveraged global developments to create new types of stratification and divisions amongst workers and the unemployed in the countries of the core and the South. Borders are being used more and more ruthlessly to police 'surplus' populations and to generate informal workforces. At the same time, neoliberalism has sharply increased the ethnic diversity of the working class in many countries. Whereas black people, Latinos and Asians made up about 15–16 per cent of workers in the US in the core sectors of production, transportation and services in 1981, by 2012 they made up around 40 per cent of each of these groups. Overall, they made up about 35 per cent of the employed working class, compared to 22 per cent for the population as a whole.[259]

What is more, they are now spread across a much wider number of sectors than in the past and are most concentrated in workplaces in urban areas. Not surprisingly, this has led to a big increase in the proportion of black people, Asians and Latinos in unions. Black people in both the US and the UK are now more likely to be in trade unions than white people.[260] This disproportionate concentration in the working class, of course, is itself a product of racism. Huge inequalities between workers based on ethnicity and gender continue and have to be actively challenged. At a time when struggles against both racism and sexism are on the rise, this location of some of the most oppressed groups at the heart of the working class brings them new sources of power and opens up explosive possibilities for struggle.

Southern storms

The impact of neoliberalism on the Global South has been devastating. It has also been contradictory. On the one hand, the opening-up of economies to the world market has decimated established industries and rural economies, creating misery on an epic scale. On the other hand, offshoring from the core, foreign direct investment and the emergence of new centres of accumulation has led to very unevenly distributed areas of new development. One of the results has been a huge growth in urban populations. The UN estimated in 2018 that 55 per cent of the world's population lives in urban areas, up from 37 per cent in 1980. Cities have grown in every continent, but the vast majority of that increase is in the so-called developing world. The trends are dramatic:

Each day some 200,000 people are added to the population of the world's cities and towns. This is 5 million a month or 60 million a year – more in one year than the 45 million added to the whole of the urban population of Europe in the whole of the 19th century.[261]

Urbanisation has various drivers. At one end of the spectrum is the pull of expanding modern industrial and service economies. The growth of Chinese industry is the most spectacular and significant example. China's share of global industrial manufacturing shot up from 8.4 per cent in 2004 to 28.7 per cent in 2019, surpassing that of the US in around 2010.[262] In the course of a generation, several hundred million former Chinese peasants have become urban workers, mostly in cities that have grown up virtually overnight. Anyone tempted to accept the hypothesis of the end of the working class needs only to glance at the figures for the size of China's manufacturing workplaces to think again. The biggest, the Longua Science and Technology Park in Shenzen which produces parts for iPhones, employs somewhere between 250,000 to 400,000 workers.[263] China is a dramatic, outlying case, but not a complete exception.

As Beverly Silver shows, the 'spatial fixes' that have been used to access cheap labour have created new or expanding working classes in other parts of the world. A few developing countries, from Brazil and South Africa to South Korea and Taiwan, that had built a reasonable economic base during the long boom, experienced 'economic miracles' at the start of the neoliberal experiment in the later 1970s and 1980s, developing internationally competitive, mass-production industries. Despite investor disappointment with India's failure to come near China's exceptional growth rates, manufacturing there has grown significantly over the last 2 decades and India's high-tech sector continues to expand. Parts of south-east Asia have also experienced significant industrialisation in the last decade, driven partly by Western outsourcing and partly by integration into expanding Asian production chains stimulated by the growing market for exports to China.[264] There are areas of new investment in most other parts of the developing world, often in Special Economic Zones, areas immune from any kind of regulatory oversight.

There is, however, a very different aspect to the urbanisation in many parts of Asia, Latin America and Africa where the opening-up of the world economy in the 1980s and 1990s led to a collapse in traditional agriculture as well as of many existing industries. In these areas there has been 'urbanisation without growth' as free-market policies, debt crises and structural adjustment programmes have devastated economies and people gravitate to the cities because life is unsustainable in the countryside. A UN report describes how in these cases, 'Instead of being a focus for growth and prosperity, the cities have become a dumping ground for a surplus population working in unskilled, unprotected and low wage informal service industries and trades.'[265]

However, the common, apocalyptic take of an urban poor cut off from the world economy and separated from a dwindling working class rarely fits the facts.[266] The 'informal economy' is a complex category in itself. Many of the small workshops and businesses that comprise it are integrated in complex ways with national and international circuits of capital giving workers in it the capacity for collective economic struggle.[267] Seasonal agricultural work that comes under this category is often essential to national economies. As Immanuel Ness argues:

The vast majority of labourers in the Global South, whether in urban settlements or rural regions, are employed under informal conditions with haphazard and irregular work hours and low wages. Workers in these regions produce a range of goods for the global commodity supply chain, whether in manufacturing, agriculture or mining. They represent the bottom of the economic ladder, but their work is crucial in creating profit for local, regional and multinational executive classes who are the recipients of surplus value from their labour.[268]

The informal economy is also never completely sealed off from what remains of traditional industrial and service sectors and also from new, outsourced enterprises or even high-investment industries. In their description of class and resistance in Soweto in South Africa, for example, Leo Zeilig and David Seddon point to the relationship between relatively secure workforces and the wider urban population, even in areas of mass unemployment, which can open up possibilities for struggle:

The jobless and formally employed are not hermetically sealed from each other, neither in terms of the household nor neighbourhood. They are not clustered in the so-called 'informal' slum settlements of Soweto. This does not imply that the effects of unemployment have not had a dramatic and devastating effect on the poor. In fact the picture derived from the survey is that most families have been shaken by the hurricane of job losses. But this has important consequences for the character and pattern of social unrest. If there is no clear divide in the world of unemployment and formal employment, then the potential for a similar crossover exists as regards popular protest and social dissidence.[269]

Seismic restructuring in the Global South has involved the dismantling of welfare and the wholesale privatisation of public enterprises and infrastructure, the accumulation by dispossession that David Harvey describes. Often this has been the result of IMF-imposed Structural Adjustment Programmes, although most of the ruling classes in developing countries have proved keen enough to participate actively. Either way, the process has taken some countries to the brink of collapse. US sanctions on some Latin American countries and direct Western military intervention, particularly in the Middle East and parts of Africa, have pushed other states into or to the edge of outright failure.

As well as traumatising whole populations, these developments have created deep crises for the left and labour organisations in parts of the Global South. Many of the most highly unionised industries and services have disappeared and much of the traditional left was orientated on attempts to control large state sectors which often no longer exist. Demoralisation and disorientation have been deepened by the fact that many of the parties most associated with state-led development were amongst the first to embrace neoliberalism. In Latin America, for example, it was the Institutional Revolutionary Party (PRI), for years the populist expression of the Mexican state, that began parcelling out state assets to multinational capital in the 1980s. In Argentina, the Perónist Carlos Menem was master of ceremonies at the great state sell-off of 1989-1990. This trend and the immense hostility shown by the US towards the Venezuelan and other 'Bolivarian' experiments in relatively mild social redistribution, indicate that the space for relatively popular or progressive nationalist governments, always limited, is closing down.

All this has led some to doubt the possibility of an agent of change emerging in the developing world. There has, however, been an impressive and often unacknowledged level of resistance to neoliberalism in different parts of the Global South, particularly in the last two decades. Three cycles of opposition in particular stand out. The first was the great wave of insurgent movements that shook parts of Latin America in the early years of this century. From 1998 to 2002, Latin America experienced its worst recession since the early days of the debt crisis. After two decades of declining living standards and broken promises this created a situation in which, in the words of one commentator, 'the chasm between the ideology of neoliberalism and the material reality facing the rural and urban popular classes became unsustainable'.[270] The left had suffered terrible defeats and the only response to crisis on offer from the elites was to complain of continued bureaucratic obstruction to structural adjustment programmes and push for more neoliberal reform.[271]

Out of this situation a re-composition of the left and the social movements emerged. The 1998 election of Hugo Chavez in Venezuela was one expression of this, but there was also an explosion of extra-parliamentary struggle across the region. This included an escalation in the campaign by the Brazilian Landless Workers Movement that mobilised tens of thousands of the country's poorest and most excluded agricultural workers, a movement in Argentina led by the unemployed 'piqueteros' that blocked major highways, occupied public buildings in a militant campaign to improve welfare, and in

Cochabamba, Bolivia's fourth city, massive protests to reverse the privatisation of the city's water supply. This insurgent campaign was led by indigenous informal workers, factory workers and peasants and mobilised pieceworkers from the sweatshops, street vendors and students from the university. Together these groups brought the city to a standstill during four days of strike action. The struggle won in the face of heavy police repression because it was beginning to draw in workers and students across the country.[272] An explosion of extra-parliamentary action followed across the region including road blockades, strikes, land occupations and worker takeovers of abandoned factories.

In Argentina, the movement headed by the piqueteros brought down the government. The Confederation of the Indigenous Nationalities of Ecuador led a broad-based insurgency there that also removed the president. Across the region, the movements began to shift from defensive struggles against the continuation of neoliberal policies towards offensive, anti-capitalist struggles consciously trying to develop strategies for socialist transition.[273]

In the context of a recovery in growth levels by 2003, the movement tended to re-orientate to electoral politics, but the ideological shift it had achieved was truly remarkable. In the first decade of this century, left or left-of-centre parties won elections in Argentina, Bolivia, Brazil, Chile, Ecuador, El Salvador, Guatemala, Nicaragua, Paraguay, Peru, Uruguay and Venezuela. And the mass struggles were far from over. One of the highpoints of the whole cycle was the 16 May 2005 Bolivian uprising demanding gas nationalisation. This time, the movement of formal and informal workers, indigenous groups and students brought the Bolivian state to the point of collapse. While 100,000 people besieged parliament, miners marched on the city of El Alto and teachers called a national strike. The opportunity may have slipped away but there is no question that on that day, a powerless government faced a mass popular movement that had brought the economy to halt and was determined, co-ordinated and calling for alternative forms of power.[274]

Just 6 years later, a second revolutionary wave engulfed large parts of North Africa and the Middle East. The Arab Spring is normally understood as a spontaneous cycle of democratic uprisings against archaic Arab authoritarianism. As a result, three aspects of the events are often ignored. The first is their economic component. The previous decade had witnessed both an acceleration in privatisation and the dismantling of the last remnants of Nasserite social provision in Egypt. The result was that the number of Egyptians living on less than two dollars a day had doubled from 20 per cent to 44 per cent, storing up huge anger at the base of society. The second aspect is their anti-imperialist backstory. The two central insurrections in the cycle, in Tunisia and Egypt, can partly be traced to the radicalising impact of the second Palestinian intifada of 2000, and the 2003 US invasion of Iraq and the worldwide resistance it triggered. Describing the transformation of the Tunisian General Workers Union (UGTT) in the first years of this century, Samni Zemni explains:

> The anti-war movement was the first area of mobilization where the union reclaimed its critical role, albeit very cautiously and within the confines of what was possible within Ben Ali's system. Just as in Morocco or Egypt, the Iraqi crisis and the plight of the Palestinians – while based on strong feelings of solidarity – were also used by local organizations to test the limits of political possibilities and as such to reveal a wider disgruntlement within the population.[275]

The other thing missing from the mainstream narrative is the role played by the working class. A worker-led rebellion against job cuts and unfair hiring practices in the rundown mining region of Gafsa in 2008 provided a crucial impulse for the Tunisian revolution. Though the insurgency was repressed, it radicalised the population and forced the UGTT centre stage. It was no accident that the massive 14 January 2011 demonstrations that forced President Ben Ali to flee the country began at the national headquarters of the UGTT.[276]

The Egyptian revolution was also foreshadowed by huge workers' struggles. In late 2006, a strike by 25,000 textile workers at the Misr Spinning and Weaving Company in Mahalla al-Kubra set off a wave of workers' mobilisations. Further strikes took place in 2008 and the working class was to play an important part in the revolutionary process. Two weeks after the first great protest in Tahrir Square, the fortunes of the revolution remained uncertain. Attacks on Tahrir had been heroically beaten off, protest had spread across the country, defence committees had emerged in poor and working-class neighbourhoods, but the government and the state remained in place. Workers' action helped to break the logjam. On Tuesday 8 February, Cairo Telecom workers, some Suez Canal staff and local steel workers went on strike. In a matter of hours, a strike wave was sweeping the country, drawing in 300,000 workers across 15 governorates. By the end of the next day, hospital technicians, postal workers, cement and textile workers had joined the action in support of the revolution, each raising new demands. Mubarak was forced out on 11 February.[277]

In both Tunisia and Egypt, workers remained important to the revolutionary process after the removal of their presidents. In Egypt in particular, workers' demands exploded. There were strikes, occupations and protests in hundreds of workplaces calling for wage rises, improved conditions, an end to corruption, and the re-employment of sacked militants. Independent unions and other new workers' organisations spread like wildfire.

Egypt's biggest paper, Al-Ahram, commented in late February:

> In one day in downtown Cairo, a passer-by could cross a
> group of workers of Nile Enterprise for Cotton staging a
> sit-in in front of the prosecutor-general's office, a group of
> teachers outside the Ministry of Education and employees of
> the recently privatised chain Omar Effendi protesting at the
> company's headquarters.[278]

Many workplaces called for the removal of top management.
Many workers' organisations also demanded the immediate
formation of a democratic government. Workers knew the army
was an enemy because it had direct interests in key sections of
industry.

One of the sources of the weakness and ultimate defeat of
the Egyptian revolution was that the power of workers was not
tied firmly enough into the revolutionary process. In the words
of the Egyptian revolutionary Sameh Naquib, 'Although the
revolution involved the rise of a militant workers' movement
clearly resonating with the democratic movement of the
squares, it remained separate from that movement. The division
between politics and economics remained largely intact.'[279] The
problem was that workers and the left didn't manage to create
institutions of struggle that could take this process forward and
allow them to start to give a lead to the rest of the oppressed. In
the absence of mass forums of workers and the poor, it was hard
to stop the initiative flowing back to the military after they had
cleared Tahrir Square.

Despite the defeat of the revolutionary wave that began in
2011, insurgent movements have re-emerged since in different
parts of the developing world in a third cycle of protest.
Conditions that led to the Arab Spring had deteriorated. Growth
in large parts of the developing world had slowed and the gap
between the north and the south had grown. These trends

intersected with the accumulated impact of Western military interventions to push more countries into permanent crisis. As a result, the year or so before the coronavirus struck was marked by huge popular movements in countries across the Middle East, the Maghreb and Latin America. In the words of *The Economist*, 'unrest and economic underperformance haunt the emerging world'.[280]

Protests in Latin America began in Argentina in September 2019 and spread the next month to Ecuador and Chile, shattering the regional elite's confidence that the region's left-wing 'pink tide' was in retreat. While all of the protests were responses to particular economic grievances, they generalised and morphed into anti-government movements with astonishing speed. In Chile, the government's retreat over price hikes on the metro only encouraged the spread of protest. A brutal police response further intensified resistance and led to organised workers taking action in support. In the Middle East and North Africa, insurgent street protest returned in 2018 and 2019 after several years of counter-revolutionary pushback against the Arab Spring. Protests in Tunisia were followed by insurgent movements in Algeria and Sudan. Both toppled their presidents. In the weeks that followed, mass struggle spread north to Iraq and Lebanon which both saw their biggest street protests for decades.

Once again, workers have played a key role in many of these struggles. This wave reached one of its high points in Sudan, one of the poorest countries of the world. Months of mass mobilisations forced President al-Bashir out in April 2019. The question then was whether the revolution would tackle wider social and democratic issues or would limit itself to the demands being put forward by the middle-class leadership of the Forces for Freedom and Change, leaving the old state essentially untouched. A possible answer was provided by a cycle of massive general strikes in May and June 2019.

A fascinating report on the June strikes by the newly formed Sudanese Professionals Association provides proof of how effective strike action can be even in the poorest countries. According to their account, 95 per cent of high schools were closed, 80-90 per cent of public road transport was stopped, 99 per cent of domestic flights, 85 per cent of sea freight, nearly 100 per cent of railway traffic, and 90 per cent of the oil and gas and the engineering sectors stopped work. The vast majority of both the sugar mills and the telecommunications sector were stopped, as were all the political and sports newspapers at least on the first day of the strike. Health workers struck across the country, 'whilst taking into consideration covering all emergency sections and cases' and keeping hospitals open. Wide sections of the middle classes were drawn into action. The report claims 100 per cent of lawyers and judges stopped work during the strike and the prosecutor's office itself was shutdown.[281]

In an interesting discussion of these events, Sudanese activist Muzan Alneel recounted that the mass strikes transformed the situation. On the one hand, they gave workers an enormous sense of confidence in their own power; on the other they laid bare the brutality of the state and its powerlessness in the face of a complete shutdown of society. The strikes contained the promise not just of replacing the government but of overthrowing the order that allows them to rule in the first place: 'The reactionary forces hate the strike, the sectarians hate it, the army hates it; they hate this weapon capable of not only overthrowing some of them, but also overthrowing the exact reasons for their existence and their privileges.'[282]

These three waves of struggle, in Latin America at the start of the century, in the Middle East and beyond from 2011, and then globally in 2019, confirm without doubt that the conditions for major revolt are in place in large parts of the developing world. They show too that despite the depredations of neoliberalism and the left's crises, effective coalitions of resistance can be built in the Global South with the potential to overthrow governments, force economic change and even challenge state power. These involved forms of working-class militancy, new and old, that proved capable of bringing capital accumulation to a halt and effectively disrupting the functioning of society. These experiences should also allay the anxieties of those who believe that alternatives to neoliberal capitalism are no longer imaginable. The great Latin American revolts at the start of the century not only threw up a series of anti-neoliberal governments, but helped kickstart an international anti-capitalist movement, popularise the slogan 'another world is possible', and generate an international debate about what it might look like.

It is not the case, then, as many fear, that the conditions for insurgent workers' struggle no longer exist in the Global South, or that alternative ways of organising society cannot emerge. Time after time, the most intractable problems that face the movements in fact concern political strategy: the question of how to move in the direction of this other world. In Sudan, the working class has played an important role in driving the revolution forward. So far, however, workers have not found a basis on which to develop an independent class policy to challenge the leadership of the Forces for Freedom and Change and impose their interests on the revolutionary process. As Alneel argues, the whole future of the revolution, even its potential to deliver democracy, depends on whether the movement finds a way to break the subordination of workers' interests and to overcome the separation of politics and economics:

We cannot repeat the failure of unprincipled coalitions. It is a folly to leave behind all this practical revolutionary knowledge we gained in the last two years and concede the idea of separating economy from politics. We would be bound then to never understand the nature of the fight and never participate in it effectively, not to mention win it.[283]

Lost legitimacy

Over the last 40 years, the ruling class has enriched itself on an undreamt-of scale, but their system has not been able to solve the central problem it confronted in the 1970s: a historically low rate of profit. As a result, their regime has generated a multi-level crisis in society. Increased exploitation has been accompanied by a frenzy of financial speculation, deeper and deeper economic crises and an accelerated assault on welfare. Far from generating a friction-free world market, as its prophets promised, globalisation has led to a renewed assault by the most powerful economies on the poor of the Global South, including the enforced opening-up of markets, all sorts of covert intervention and open military assault. The results have included millions of dead, a string of failed states, and forced migrations on a scale never known before. Meanwhile, the pandemics and the existential threat of climate crisis have revealed that an unplanned and rapacious relationship with our environment can only end in disaster.

Despite this, neoliberal ideas have proved remarkably resilient in official society. In politics and the state, in the media, in academia and in mainstream intellectual life in general any challenge to pro-market fatalism is still regarded as eccentric. Given their identification with socialist ideas, it is perhaps no surprise that Corbyn and Sanders were both treated as political imposters, and dangerous ones at that. Even the mildest support for social planning as anything more than a temporary expedient is still treated as an affront to the natural laws of supply and demand, and the necessity of a balanced budget.

As we shall see, continued ruling-class commitment to the neoliberal agenda has real macroeconomic foundations. The extreme lack of dissenting voices in the mainstream is, however, partly a result of the neoliberal reorganisation of the state. Business and state institutions have integrated to a degree not captured by the cliché of the 'revolving door'.

Governments have stuffed top layers of the civil service with industry professionals for their private-sector experience, their influence within corporations and in order to gain political support from private firms. Industry, in turn, has hired people from government positions as policy to gain personal access to government officials, to push for favourable legislation and government contracts. This process has helped turn what used to be called corruption into a system of government.

The longevity of neoliberal 'thought' is also the product of one more important development of the last few decades: the enormous enrichment of the upper levels of the professional and managerial classes. The claim, fashionable on the left, that society is essentially divided between the bottom 99 percent and the top 1 per cent obscures this important class dynamic. As Thomas Piketty has shown, in the advanced countries the share of total private property and income in the hands of the top 10 per cent has grown as fast and in some cases faster than that of the top 1 per cent since 1980. In Europe, by no means the most unequal region of the world, the top ten per cent now owns between 50 and 60 per cent of total wealth.[284]

In other parts of the world, including for example India and Russia, the rise has been even more dramatic.[285] In the Middle East, the most unequal region on earth, on average the top 10 per cent earn fully 63 per cent of total income.[286] Whereas, historically at least, sections of the better-off professional and middle classes have solidarized with working people, their attitudes have decisively changed as their fortunes have diverged sharply from those of the majority of working people. In the context of a low level of working-class struggle and the capitulation of social democracy to the market, their rapidly increasing wealth has tied them to a toxic status quo and encouraged them to reproduce variations of their rulers' worldview. In the words of Catherine Liu's withering take on the 'Professional Managerial Class' in the US:

The PMC is deeply hostile to simple redistributive policies that a Bernie Sanders presidency would have implemented: it is against the idea of building solidarity among the oppressed. It prefers obscurantism, balkanisation, and management of interest groups to a transformative reimagination of the social order. It wants to play the virtuous social hero, but as a class, it is hopelessly reactionary. The interests of the PMC are now tied more than ever to its corporate overlords than to the struggles of the majority of Americans whose suffering is merely background décor for the PMC's elite volunteerism.[287]

As a result, many on the left fear that neoliberal thinking has come to dominate society completely. Pierre Dardot and Christian Laval put the case strongly in their 2009 book *The New Way of the World,* arguing that neoliberalism had generated a 'new rationality' that had penetrated so deep not just into institutions but into the collective psyche that it had become a 'world reason'.[288] The reality has turned out to be rather different.

Neoliberal dogma has indeed captured the thinking of many of those who run key institutions, the universities, the media, even the remnants of the welfare state and the health service. It therefore has an influence on all layers in society and can appear to be pervasive, depending on the circles in which you move. Rarely, however, has it come near to dominating popular consciousness. Polls in country after country, including the US, repeatedly show that majorities see inequality as a major problem, want increased spending on health and education, and support trade unions, in other words dissent comprehensively from the 'world reason' of the globalisers.[289]

Despite the stereotypes promoted by 'enlightened' elites, research overviews show that the working poor tend to have the most progressive attitudes on social issues.[290] Even at the height of Thatcher's success in 1987, the British Social Attitudes Survey showed that more than three-quarters of the population thought that 'the nation's wealth is shared unfairly', 54 per cent that 'big business benefits owners at the expense of workers', and 59 per cent that 'there is one law for the rich and another for the poor'. As John Curtice, one of the editors, concluded, 'Within the working class there is a large majority with radical or egalitarian views.'[291]

In fact, in the last decade or so, massive numbers of people have come to the conclusion that capitalism is a problem and even to self-identify as socialists. According to a 2021 report published by the right-wing thinktank the Institute for Economic Affairs, nearly 80 per cent of younger Britons blame capitalism for the housing crisis, 75 per cent believe the climate emergency is 'specifically a capitalist problem' and 72 per cent back sweeping nationalisation. Overall, 67 per cent want to live under a socialist economic system. To make matters worse for the establishment, the figures are not so different for other age groups.[292] On the other side of the Atlantic, a Harvard University study in 2016 found that more than 50 per cent of young people in the heartland of laissez-faire economics reject capitalism.[293]

This is, of course, because it is more than anything the experience of reality that shapes people's ideas. In Marx's words, 'being determines consciousness', and the lived reality of neoliberalism for working people around the globe has been the direct opposite of that of the small minority it has so spectacularly enriched. The fact that neoliberalism's key institutions are run by such firm defenders of the status quo may have given it an extra lease of life and caused some confusion on the left, but at a certain point being so out of touch with popular experience becomes a liability for any regime. One recent international survey of trust in institutions warned that more than half of respondents believed that capitalism in its current form is now doing more harm than good in the world.

Despite a strong global economy and near full employment, none of the institutions that the study measured, government, business, NGOs and media, is trusted. The result of record inequality, is, it said:

> ...a world of two different trust realities. The informed public –wealthier, more educated, and frequent consumers of news – remain far more trusting of every institution than the mass population. In a majority of markets, less than half of the mass population trust their institutions to do what is right.[294]

6. Conclusion: The Return of the Repressed?

The first claim of this book is that despite the protestations of journalists, experts, academics, politicians of all parties and a surprising number of left-wing commentators, class has always been and remains the defining division in capitalism. This is because it is the key relation enabling the accumulation of profit by the capitalist class. It is the inescapable social expression of the fact that the tiny minority who own and run business extract their wealth from the majority by forcing them to work, to labour, under their control and for their benefit.

As we have seen, the establishment has downplayed the idea of class since the mid-nineteenth century when working-class organisation first became a threat. As capitalism consolidated its hold, however, society continued to resolve itself into a tiny class of capital owners and a mass of wage earners from whom they extract profit. The working class expanded dramatically in the late nineteenth century. It grew again after both world wars and rapidly during the long boom of the 1950s and 1960s. By the 1980s, there were more workers in South Korea than there were in the whole world when Marx was alive.[295] In large parts of the world, the independent peasantry has now disappeared. The middle classes of Marx's day have been transformed to include wider layers of managers and professionals. They are essential to the functioning of the system, but their role is precisely to manage and facilitate the driving process of the economy, the accumulation of profit from the labour of wage earners, now the majority around the world. Marx's forecast of the division of society into two, *main* classes has been borne out.

Despite the chorus of denial, the process has continued during the neoliberal years. The search for profits has led to a massive restructuring of the global economy, but this economy is still driven mainly by the production and sale of commodities. There has been a corporate takeover of parts of the welfare state and other state-run sectors. Insofar as this represents 'accumulation through dispossession', however, these are one-off gains. Capitalists have found other novel ways to capture and even expand value in the short term. The process of privatisation has been accompanied by a massive increase in private debt and an associated increase in the amount of capital tied up in finance and financial instruments, what Marx called 'fictitious capital'. While they provide outlets for capital looking for opportunities, however, these things are not a long-term alternative to exploitation at the point of production.

Surplus value still accrues mainly from the unique capacity of human labour to transform the world, to add value. An economy that expands way beyond the bounds of the production of actual surplus value will in the end suffer a destabilising correction, just as it did in 2008. The production of commodities through exploitation remains in other words the driving force of the system. As a result, working people continue to have unmatched potential power to disrupt. From sprawling hi-tech manufacturing plants in Shenzen, Bangalore or Seattle to the massive garment factories of Bangladesh and Vietnam, from logistic hubs, retail parks, to call centres, schools, universities and hospitals all around the world, the scale and complexity of our globalised, just-in-time economy means workers maintain the capacity to bring the system to a standstill.

The book's second contention is connected to the first. It is that class struggle has played a much more important role during the relatively short history of capitalism than is normally admitted. The period after the First World War witnessed by far the deepest and most sustained working-class insurgencies in history. The fallout shaped politics until the Second World War and the experience continued to haunt the ruling class in the years after. But it is simply not true, as many even on the left suggest, that working-class challenges to the capitalist order have been confined to the inter-war years. As we have seen, there were moments at the end of the Second World War and during the post-1968 period when workers' self-activity threatened capitalist continuity in various countries in the core and beyond. Even though it was successfully contained, workers' struggle played an essential role in the victory of many anti-colonial movements around the world.

All this explains why the 1970s New Right set itself the task of eradicating the class consciousness and combativity that pervaded wide sections of the working population. After years of defeat, traditions of working-class struggle have since been rediscovered; for example, in the great upheavals that rocked Bolivia, Ecuador, Venezuela and Argentina at the start of this century, and they have reappeared in the global cycle of upheavals in both 2011 and 2019. Even in quieter periods in which expert commentators have announced a truce between the classes or the disappearance of class altogether, class struggle continues, 'now open, now hidden' as Marx argued, storing up stresses in the system that eventually tend to burst into open battle.

Capitalism and consciousness

The current prejudice is that working people tend to be more socially conservative, backward and 'nativist' than other groups. My third contention is that in reality, throughout most of the period I have discussed, the working class has been the most important source of radical ideas in society. Socialism emerged as the collective aspiration of militant working people in the second half of the nineteenth century and touched the lives of workers everywhere. Its revolutionary variant haunted political and social life from 1917 until the Second World War. Various forms of socialist ideas dominated post-war politics and came to the fore again in the great explosions of the 1960s and 1970s. Even at times of relative social peace or working-class defeat, class consciousness has proved resilient and the numbers of people who self-define as working class often surprise.

We have seen that neither the boom years of alleged class compromise nor the open class assault of the last few decades resulted in the eradication of class-based attitudes. The steady rightward shift of social democracy during the post-war boom was matched by depoliticisation amongst workers but also the stubborn survival of 'us and them'. Thatcherism failed to eradicate redistributive prejudices amongst workers. A recent British study charting the 'decline of deference' between 1968 and 2000 noted that class continued to be a key preoccupation throughout the period and that people never stopped using class to place themselves in society. It also suggested that as deference to the elites declined, socially egalitarian attitudes which had always been widespread amongst the core of the working class spread to much wider sectors of society.[296]

Another case that this book has made, however, is that the political ideas and traditions influencing working-class organisations have been important and often decisive to the outcomes of struggles. The role of political ideas in collective struggle is often downplayed and the openness of historical moments ignored or forgotten. Debates within the working-class movement are rarely of much interest to academic historians. This lack of interest, and a tendency to retrospective fatalism in writing history, has been reinforced by the mechanical materialism so influential in Marxism at various times.

Such closure often serves particular political interests. Post-colonial elites regularly pleaded, for example, that their regimes were unable to deliver for their populations because the material conditions for socialism were not present.[297] As I have shown, questions of politics and organisation in fact played an important role in shaping post-colonial outcomes.

Fatalism returns in new forms. In the early 1980s, the theorists of New Times pretty much avoided any discussion of political organisation or strategy by putting victories of the New Right down to the development of new forms of production, consumption and 'hegemonic cultures'.[298] This was to ignore the reality that the ideas and strategies that informed the mainstream left at the time had played into the right's rise.

Of course, the objective social relations and the balance of class forces at particular times and places set the limits of the possible. The issue here, however, is not just whether *particular opportunities* were missed due to the insufficient weight of revolutionary forces or ideas. It is also about how various organisations and ideas, and the victories or defeats they preside over, shape developments over time. One of my arguments in this book, for example, has been that the dominance of reformist and Stalinist politics in the European working class in the years after the war helped contain a number of potentially revolutionary situations. The wider point, however, is that those setbacks also had a disorientating impact on the working class for years afterwards. Similarly, the attacks on working-class living standards by social-democratic governments and the move away from class politics in the 1970s helped both to enable the rise of the New Right and to sow confusion in the working-class movement for decades.

Foregrounding the importance of political ideas and organisation in working-class politics might seem to contradict the earlier emphasis on experience in shaping workers' ideas and on the resilience of class consciousness. This, however, is a contradiction that exists in the real world, and it was precisely the issues it throws up that Antonio Gramsci and Georg Lukács explored in their post-revolutionary reflections. They saw that life under capitalism spontaneously generates *both* a level of class consciousness *and* that that consciousness needs to be actively, collectively developed. Workers have an interest in critiquing and challenging capitalism. This is why Lukács argued that the working class was both the subject and the object of its knowledge. In his own words:

> for the proletariat the total knowledge of its class situation was a vital necessity, a matter of life and death; because its class situation becomes comprehensible only if the whole of society can be understood; and because this understanding is the inescapable precondition of its actions. Thus the unity of theory and practice is only the reverse side of the social and historical position of the proletariat. From its own point of view self-knowledge coincides with knowledge of the whole so that the proletariat is at one and the same time the subject and object of its own knowledge.[299]

The position of the working class in society provides a standpoint and a social basis from which to launch a defence of universality and a critique of those who say that the world cannot be understood, let alone fundamentally transformed. The process of workers acquiring self-knowledge, however, is not automatic and can only be an active one, both intellectually and practically. To believe otherwise would be to succumb once again to fatalism, to the idea that change happens independently of human action. As Stephen Perkins puts it in his commentary on Lukács:

> The notion that that society is governed by extra-human laws, whether these justify the eternal existence of capitalism or indicate its inevitable demise, is a self-validating intellectual exercise rejected by both Lukács and Marx...such a notion is encouraged and strengthened by the conditions of life in capitalist society; it is also perhaps the primary guarantee of the ideological hegemony and continued reproduction of that system of society.[300]

This brings us to the central paradox shaping working-class life and thought. Capitalist production is both the source of class struggle and resistance and at the same time the central point of domination of labour and the working class by capital. It was the implications of this apparent paradox that Antonio Gramsci and Georg Lukács explored in their writings in the aftermath of the Russian Revolution. Their ideas are important because, based as they were on experience of the highest points of working-class struggle, they take us beyond the kind of one-sided discussions about consciousness that tend to dominate today's left.

In general, the left tends to focus on the power of propaganda, the media, education, prejudice and often consumerism to confuse the mass of the population. This is because downplaying class leads people to miss the source of radicalisation at the heart of capitalist society. In different ways, Gramsci and Lukács saw that capitalism has the tendency at different times *both* to conceal its own real relations *and* to radicalise working people. Gramsci recognised the way struggle could transform people's understanding of the world but also explored the way the traditional institutions and ideas of class society can inhibit the development of a clear class consciousness. Lukács rooted the two sides of mass consciousness more comprehensively in the economic structures of capitalism. Building on Marx's insights, he pointed out that the system itself generates anger and opposition, but the alienated nature of production and the reification it produces can create a sense of powerlessness and limit people's ability to grasp the robbery at the heart of the process. The result, enhanced by the efforts of bourgeois ideologists, is that working people have what Gramsci called a 'contradictory consciousness'.

The fact that capitalism is based on exploitation ensures that there is always opposition to class rule. The constant conflict between boss and worker produces some level of class consciousness *at all times*: a feeling of us and them; hatred of the boss; sympathy with or participation in unions; votes for social democrats and so on. In this sense, Marx was right to say there is always class struggle and class consciousness. It is built into class society. It is, however, normally limited, compromised, held back from revolutionary conclusions by the experience of alienation and powerlessness. Mass struggles can do a lot to break down illusions. Resisting wage cuts or speed-ups or fire and rehire involves a struggle over the terms of exploitation. When the struggle takes a sharp form, it can begin to reveal that there is an irreconcilable opposition between the interests of workers and bosses. When struggle spreads, various institutions of the state can intervene, politicising the dispute and exposing the fact that the whole edifice of official society is rigged against workers and is based on the commodification of everything.

For both Gramsci and Lukács, as for Marx, this tendency to generalisation is greater in periods of economic crisis. At these moments, in Lukács' words: 'The unity of the economic process now moves within reach.'[301] All the same, even at times of deep crisis and mass working-class resistance, the hold of the old ideas, assumptions and organisation are not automatically broken. There is instead an ideological crisis in the working class because in some ways workers remain caught up in capitalist ways of thought and feeling. What is often an extremely precarious position for the ruling class can remain endowed in the minds of workers 'with all its erstwhile stability'. At the same time, the established organisations of the working class, committed in general to sectional struggles and reform within the system, actively work to try and ensure that spontaneous actions of the working class remain on the level of pure spontaneity:

They strive to prevent them from turning their attention to the totality, whether this be territorial, professional, etc., or whether it involves synthesising the economic movement with the political one.[302]

Trade unions, of course, remain essential in these circumstances as the basic units of working-class organisation and their reach will be a decisive factor in any major struggle. Working-class politics however can't be reduced to building union strength. Unions are deeply shaped by their role in capitalist society. Their sectionalism reflects rather than challenges the various forms of division within the process of production. Their leaderships, whose role in society is to negotiate the terms of exploitation, industry by industry, will in general oppose calls for workers' control and the root-and-branch transformation of society. At high points in working-class struggle, rank-and-file organisations of various kinds are necessary to overcome sectionalism and to ensure that workers' aspirations are not limited by the perspectives of the union full timers. Reformist political organisations, meanwhile, will continue to have a strong influence even at times of major struggle, and their promotion of gradualism and compromise needs to be actively challenged.

This is why Gramsci, Lukács, Lenin, Luxemburg, and others in the twentieth-century classical Marxist tradition saw that the full development of class consciousness requires specific, revolutionary organisation. Such organisation is designed to hold on to and develop the insights gained by the most conscious workers at the height of struggles, to generalise them as widely as possible and to overcome sectionalism and gradualism. This is not just a question of technically preparing a revolution, or of spreading socialist propaganda and ideas, however important these things may be. To believe so is just the other side of the idea that revolution is a matter of a spontaneous 'break' or 'event', a fashionable notion today amongst some on the academic left.[303] Lukács stressed that Lenin always understood revolution as a process in which the subjective and the objective *interact over time.* Revolutionary organisation is necessary actively to develop the situation; 'to accelerate the maturing of these revolutionary tendencies by its actions'.[304]

Focussed as they are on elections, reformist organisations take a snapshot of public opinion, or at best of the opinions of working people, and adapt to it. Revolutionary socialist organisation has fundamentally different aims and methods. It aims to relate at all times to the most active and militant members of the working class, to try and offer leadership to those struggles which do take place and to draw socialist conclusions out of those struggles. This involves bringing together the most radical workers around a set of principles. It implies a certain political separation from the rest of the working class, but only so that the most clear-sighted workers can campaign to persuade others that their principles are correct. The ultimate aim is to overcome division and oppression, to unite workers in an active assault on the system. But the paradox is that unity has to be campaigned for. And just as reformism takes organisational form, so must revolutionary politics, or else it can have no impact.

As well as forming a revolutionary core and putting political arguments, socialists, however, always need to try to reach out and organise joint *action* with wider groups still under the influence of reformist ideas. When effective, such action, whether it takes the form of united-front campaigns or workplace-based rank-and-file organisation, weakens the position of the employing class and increases the confidence, combativity and clarity of all those involved in the struggle. To make a difference to the world and to resist the dangers of incorporation, revolutionary organisation has to be built on the dynamic intersection between existing struggles and theoretical foresight. As Gramsci argued, 'It is not a question of introducing from scratch a scientific form of thought into everyone's individual life, but of renovating and making "critical" an already existing activity.'[305] Only in this way can the accumulated lessons of revolutionary history be brought to bear decisively on the present to shape the future.

Existence and resistance now

We have seen that many on the left have tended to emphasise the disorientating, atomising impact of neoliberal capitalism on workers' consciousness. The view from the left in the academy was encapsulated by Frederic Jameson's turn-of-the century complaint, 'It is easier to imagine the end of the world than the end of capitalism.'[306] Jameson's pessimistic take, however, involves a one-sided understanding of the impact of commodification.

The experiment in what Andrew Glyn memorably called 'capitalism unleashed' has been a disaster for the vast majority. It has turned many people's working life into a waking nightmare, generated almost unimaginable inequality and for the first time since the Second World War led to a decline in standards of living and life expectancy for billions in the developed and underdeveloped world. It has created failing states across swathes of the globe and pushed ecological damage to a critical point. Fearful of a backlash, ruling classes around the world have resorted to authoritarianism, nationalism and racism to try and stabilise their rule without fundamentally altering the economic model. This has boosted networks of far-right and fascist groups in their efforts to turn anger and alienation against the most vulnerable. As well as creating immense misery, however, the neoliberal decades have generated significant radicalisation and opposition.

As it happens, at the very same time as Jameson was complaining that people couldn't think beyond capitalism, large numbers around the world were coming together in street protests, huge forums and direct actions in what was called the anti-capitalist movement. Its main slogan was 'our world is not for sale', but the movement also insisted precisely that 'another world is possible'. These anti-capitalist gatherings, themselves partly generated by rebellions in the developing world, were a launchpad for the global anti-war movement. This produced the biggest co-ordinated protest in human history when in 2003 an estimated 30 million people marched against the Iraq War in 600 cities around the world and helped generate a worldwide solidarity movement for Palestine. Since then as we have seen, there have been waves of global protest against austerity, the climate catastrophe and most recently unprecedented levels of international protest against systemic racism.

These movements have had successes, in some cases blocking serious attacks, in all cases raising awareness. While the anti-war movement failed to stop the first Western wars of this century, by US and British generals' own admission, it has made it extremely difficult for the Western military to even contemplate further boots-on-the ground offensives.[307] Last decade's anti-austerity mobilisations sometimes shook governments, often changed the terms of the argument and helped generate a series of radical political initiatives. The Black Lives Matter mobilisations have demoralised racists inside and outside of the police, forced the conviction of a US police officer for a racist murder, and boosted anti-racists everywhere. The mass mobilisations over climate change have brought the issue centre stage and put climate deniers on the defensive.

These street campaigns draw people into activity, raise confidence, prove that victories can be won, and radicalise people. They have generated widespread debate and discussion on issues that our rulers would much rather ignore. As well as sparking mass protest on particular issues, the sheer range and scale of the attacks on life conditions caused by rampant commodification and its champions has encouraged political generalisation. From the moment anti-capitalism went mainstream at the Seattle protests in 1999 to the Spanish Movement of the Squares in 2011 and the anti-Trump demonstrations later in the decade, the linking of different issues has become standard in twenty-first-century movements.

Despite the gloomy prognoses of Jameson and so many left intellectuals, these kinds of campaigns have also tended to kick start the discussion of alternatives. Whatever their limitations may be, the recent cycle of left governments in Latin America were an outcome of turn-of-the century mass movements. In Greece the 2015 Syriza government stemmed directly from the country's anti-austerity movement.[308] Famously, Corbynism in Britain couldn't have happened without the mass movements against war and austerity.[309] It is not then that the experience of neoliberalism has failed to generate opposition or a mass desire for change in various places. Once again the problem has often been more one of strategy and politics. In general the mass movements have found their political expression in *electoral* alternatives, and the pursuit of parliamentary means to turn back the neoliberal tide has had mixed results at best. The hopes generated across Europe by Syriza's stunning 2015 victory were crushed when the party capitulated to the demands of the 'Troika', the European Commission, the European Central Bank and the International Monetary Fund. In Britain the establishment managed to snuff out the Corbynite upsurge despite the fact that the Corbyn-led Labour Party won 13 million votes in the 2017 election, recording the biggest percentage-point increase in vote share in a single general election since 1945. Other European attempts over the last few decades to channel anger at austerity into radical electoral politics have been disappointing. Left parties of various sorts have fared much better in Latin America. As we have seen they have won elections in a host of countries including recently in Chile and Honduras. At times over the last 25 years Latin American left governments have become important points of resistance to US imperialism and neoliberal economics. Despite making real social progress in places, however, nowhere have they come near to solving the deep social problems of their countries' populations.

As Lenin himself insisted, parliamentary politics will always be important in democracies even during revolutionary periods, and the radical left should never ignore the parliamentary terrain. Given the establishment's recent success in derailing radical left projects, however, and the tendency for the social movements to vacate the streets once such projects are up and running, it is beyond time for a strategic reassessment. Focussing the growing radicalisation in society on a politics centred on class offers a way forward. Certainly, one of the strategic prizes for the left at the moment must be to find ways to link the diverse and political movements for change to the potential power of organised and organising workers. Both sides benefit from such an interaction when it happens; the political movements help to overcome sectionalism and economic narrowness in the workplaces, and workers' organisation brings social weight and new strategic possibilities to the movements. The potential for campaigns against war, austerity and climate change would be transformed if they could become more centred on workplace power.

Such a strategy of linking the political mass movements to promising shoots of union resistance isn't universally recognised as the best way forward. It points in a rather different direction, for example, to the focus on the nuts and bolts work of union organisers advocated by Jane McAlevey and others and to the fashionable ideas of using political leverage to win disputes.[310] All union organising should be welcomed, all strategies are worth trying. As the brief histories outlined in this book show, however, the great waves of working-class struggle of the past have always been linked to wider social and political crises. Given the scale and often the political nature of the assaults working people face, and the widespread radicalisation amongst them, McAlevey's advice to separate 'organising' from 'mobilising' seems counterintuitive.[311] Workplace activists cannot in fact afford to ignore wider political questions and mobilisations. In Britain, workers' ability to defend themselves industrially is being heavily circumscribed by existing trade union laws, and further threatened by new legislation. There are important political campaigns against these attacks and trade unionists need to be part of them. In France on the other hand workers won their most important recent victory by defeating Macron's assault on pension rights precisely through a combination of strikes and mass mobilisations. This national, political success has boosted workers confidence to fight on local, economic issues. Given the scale of the crises we face, relating workplace organising to the growing struggles for social change is surely a necessity, not a luxury.

The limits of identity

Not all contemporary radical politics tends towards generalisation, however. The situation is contradictory and the extreme atomisation and reification of the neoliberal years and low levels of specifically class-based struggle have inevitably had an impact. In tension with the mood for generalisation, there is also a strong contemporary tendency to focus on the *particularity of experience* rather than seeking common ground and understanding oppression as structural. All confident assertions of identity by oppressed groups or individuals raise some kind of challenge to the prevailing set up. But though identity politics started out as an attempt to force marginalised experiences into the mainstream, it has often led to the prioritisation of personal experience over general understanding. As Asad Haider argues in his assessment of contemporary identity politics, on its own, the assertion of identity risks leaving the sources of oppression unanalysed:

It is based on the individual's demand for recognition and it takes that individual's identity as its starting point. It takes this identity for granted and suppresses the fact that all identities are socially constructed. And because all of us necessarily have identities that are different from everyone else's, it undermines the possibility of collective self-organisation. The framework of identity reduces politics to who you are as an individual and to gaining recognition as an individual, rather than your membership in a collectivity and the collective struggle against an oppressive social system.[312]

Without any guiding take on the power structure of wider society, a politics of identity can lead in self-defeating directions. Writing in the 1960s, soon after desegregation had opened up some space for black professionals, managers and business people, Black Panther Huey Newton warned that black identity or nationalism can be harnessed by the emerging black elite to take control of the radical movement and suppress the demands of black working people who in reality had very different interests.[313] As Keeanga-Yamahtta Taylor points out in her discussion of the murder of Freddie Gray and the revolt that followed in Baltimore in 2015, this process has come on leaps and bounds:

There have always been class differences amongst African Americans, but this is the first time those class differences have been expressed in the form of a minority of Blacks wielding significant political power and authority over the majority of Black lives. This raises critical questions about the role of the Black elite in the continuing freedom struggle – and about what side are they on. This is not an overstatement. When a Black Mayor, governing a largely Black city, aids in the mobilization of a military unit led by a

Black woman to suppress a black rebellion, we are in a new
period of the Black freedom struggle.[314]

The struggles for civil rights and multiculturalism have won
vital victories and raised all kinds of possibilities. In the context
of neoliberalism and the growth of a wealthy managerial elite
that likes to pride itself on its inclusive values, those victories
risk being reduced to what Catherine Liu has called 'identity
protocols'; the roll out of diversity training and quotas for top
jobs. This is fine for the tiny majority of people from oppressed
groups who make it into elite jobs, and it is of course important
that such opportunities are widened. Experience in the US,
Britain and elsewhere has shown, however, that having more
women, trans people or people of colour in positions of power
and influence does next to nothing for the lives of the majority
of the oppressed. They continue to suffer structural racism,
sexism and discrimination. The system that generates these
oppressions and the exploitation at its heart go unchallenged and
is even perhaps strengthened by being able to appear inclusive.
Amongst the newly enriched professional and managerial class
(PMC) the stress on race and gender discrimination has become
a useful mechanism for both virtue signalling and deflecting
concerns about class inequality. In the words of Catherine Liu:

> As a class, the PMC loves to talk about bias rather than
> inequality, racism rather than capitalism, visibility rather
> than exploitation. Tolerance for them is the highest secular
> virtue – but tolerance has almost no political or economic
> meaning.[315]

Such diversification of the elites is welcome, but without a
challenge to the fundamental economic structures of society, it
also opens up space for the right to make headway with its own
brands of identity politics. These involve protesting against the

alleged abandonment of white workers and defending national culture and traditions against liberal, multicultural elites. In this situation the left needs to develop an independent politics that fights for oppressed groups more effectively and as a whole, but also provides a way forward for working people in general.

Dealing with class as another 'intersecting' identity doesn't solve the problem. This is because the very existence of class contains an implicit critique of existing society, not just of inequality, but of the robbery that creates it and the oppressions it generates. Recognising one's membership of the working class involves the beginnings of understanding the way the system operates as a whole. It therefore opens the possibility of *moving beyond* identities which are inevitably framed mainly by the prevailing system. One indication of this universality is that the working class contains within it the overwhelming majority of the oppressed and therefore provides at least the possibility of a fighting unity in practice.

As we have seen, however, the potential of the working class to develop a holistic understanding of the world has deeper sources. For workers, overcoming divisions of race, sex or gender is a matter of strategic urgency. The relentless exploitation they experience also gives workers a unique vantage point from which to understand the fundamental drives of the system, 'to see society from the centre as a coherent whole'.[316] Recognising this doesn't mean reducing every aspect of society to class. In fact, it means the very opposite. Whereas the ruling class needs to do everything possible to obscure the way society operates, for the working class, a complete understanding of all the complexities of capitalism is essential for achieving fundamental social change, for liberating itself.

Such holistic understanding doesn't emerge automatically. The division of labour, the reified nature of work and the fact that workers produce a whole social world that they do not control create limits to understanding most of the time. It means

156

there are always possibilities for our rulers to open up divisions in our ranks. But as we have seen, against all the stereotypes, on many issues workers' consciousness runs ahead of other classes in society even at times of relative social peace. As the primary objects of a more and more exploitative system, the working class provides a baseline of opposition to the depredations of turbocharged capitalism from which effective resistance can be launched. If socialism is about pursuing the hunch that humans could actually take control of our own destiny, then socialists need to be organised in the workplace, in the communities, alongside those people resisting. They need to be not just propagandising about the iniquities of the system but working with others to take the movement forward, not just talking about revolution but 'accelerating the maturing of…revolutionary tendencies' and at the same time helping people to understand the significance of their actions.[317]

Dominant, not leading

Given the disasters created by neoliberal capitalism, there has been speculation that ruling classes will move towards new, less toxic models of capital accumulation. There has been talk about the return of Keynesianism, protectionism and state intervention. For some, this promises the possibility of a parliamentary left once again finding the space to pursue redistribution and stimulus in government. While such developments would be welcome, they do not seem very likely. First, the sheer scale of integration of national economies around the world means that any serious attempts to implement state-driven economic development through protectionism would lead to enormous disruption across the system as a whole. They would be opposed by the majority of big capitalists who remain deeply committed to the globalised economy. In such a connected world economy, national Keynesianism is widely regarded by the elites as self-defeating, as domestic fiscal stimulus benefits foreign trading partners without their having to pay for it.[318]

Another obstacle to a return to Keynesianism is the continuing low rate of profit. As we entered the pandemic in 2020, both growth rates and profit rates were at historic lows across the system. According to the Federal Bank, US non-financial profit rates were at 3.5 compared to a peak of 8 per cent in 1966.[319] This means that the pressure to cut welfare and wages is acute everywhere, the opposite of the situation in the post-war period in which boom conditions encouraged a focus on holding on to skilled workers, conceding to strikes and paying out for limited welfare to secure social peace.

There have recently been periods of very high state spending. Famously billions were spent bailing out the banks after the 2008 banking crisis. This was a product of another one of the system's problems, that large chunks of capital are simply too big to fail. This is a fact which closes off one of the traditional solutions to a low rate of profit: letting sections of capital go to the wall. By paralysing the economy, the pandemic has forced another round of public spending in most economies. None of this signals a conversion to Keynesianism, however. Governments are still committed to long-term cuts in expenditure on education, health and social services in order to pay for these short-term economic boosts.

As a result, ruling classes around the world are discredited in the eyes of whole populations. We are moving into the kind of situation which Antonio Gramsci called 'a crisis of authority', in which ruling classes in many places no longer have active popular consent, are no longer leading, 'only "dominant"'.[320] Their wars have caused chaos and carnage across whole regions. Their economic system has failed twice over, even in its own terms. Far from trickling down, wealth is being sucked from working populations and working-class communities into the hands of an unimaginably rich ruling class and their more and more remote enablers.

Rather than leading to increased efficiency, the last 40 years of neoliberal capitalism have underlined the chaos caused by competitive accumulation. In the Global South states are failing, in the so-called heartlands more and more people can't get a home, enough food, medical essentials. In many countries, the pandemic revealed that neoliberalism's obsession with the market has eroded the most basic capacity of governments to formulate plans and implement them coherently. Competition is more and more turning to war. The climate emergency has shown that world leaders are incapable of effective co-operation even in the face of an existential threat to humanity.

These crises have helped illuminate how the system works and how it breaks. In particular, they have shown that society only continues to function because of 'key workers': transport workers, cleaners, retail staff, teachers and lecturers, hospital workers, manufacturing workers, agricultural workers, cleansing workers, IT workers, call-centre workers, care workers. The working class, to call it by its collective name. Lacking a plan B, our rulers will continue to respond to the crisis with austerity, increased repression and by trying to impose all kinds of divisions and imagined communities on the population. Our answer must be to make every effort to unite in the community they fear most.

Further Reading

As the kind of arguments made in this book are so often overlooked, it seemed sensible to provide readers with a short selection of key texts. *The German Ideology* and the *Communist Manifesto* are the best starting points for Marx's theory of class. The earlier *Economic and Philosophical Manuscripts* is dense but holds the keys to the theory of alienation. Marx's French historical studies, *Class Struggles in France* and the *Civil War in France,* show the power of Marxist class analysis in action. The three volumes of *Capital* of course provide the most complete outline of Marx's conception of how capitalist society functions and contain innumerable detailed insights about class. Hal Draper provides an extremely useful compendium of Marx's views on class in *Karl Marx's Theory of Revolution: The Politics of Social Classes.*

Three major twentieth century works are central to this book's approach to class struggle, class consciousness and revolution: Trotsky's *History of the Russian Revolution,* Lukacs's *History and Class Consciousness* and Gramsci's *Prison Notebooks.* Gramsci's *Notebooks* were produced in conditions of censorship and not for publication. As a result they are fragmentary and in places ambiguous but they contain important insights. To these should be added Rosa Luxemburg's much shorter but highly suggestive *The Mass Strike.*

Important later texts on the relationship between class and class consciousness include Franz Jakubowski's *Ideology and Superstructure in Historical Materialism*, which is a good introduction to the subject, Michael Lowy's *The Theory of Revolution in the Young Marx,* John Rees's *Algebra of Revolution,* and Stephen Perkins', *Marx and the Proletariat: A Lukacsian*

Perspective. I have written a very brief introduction to the Lukacs of the revolutionary years, *Capitalism and Class Consciousness: The Ideas of Georg Lukacs.*

Amongst the most successful more recent attempts to develop, update and apply Marx's analysis of class are Harry Braverman's *Labour and Monopoly Capitalism*, Lindsey German's *A Question of Class*, and *Class Wealth and Power in Neoliberal Britain* and Kim Moody's *On New Terrain*. Raju Das's *Marxist Class Theory in a Skeptical World* is a monumental and extremely detailed argument for the relevance of Marx's analysis of class today. Kevin Doogan very effectively takes apart the industry of class denial in *New Capitalism? The Transformation of Work*, while Beverly Silver's *Forces of Labour* has a rather different frame of analysis to mine but contains the results of important empirical research and much suggestive analysis.

Lindsey German's *Sex Class and Socialism*, Heather Brown's *Marx on Gender and the Family*, Kevin Ovenden's *Malcom X*, Keeanga-Yamahatta Taylor's *From #BlackLivesMatter to Black Liberation*, Asad Haider's *Mistaken Identity* and Kevin Anderson's *Marx at the Margins,* all contain useful discussions of the relationship between class and oppression in capitalist society.

There is only space to mention a tiny selection of relevant history writing. E.P. Thompson's *The Making of The English Working Class* is indispensable even if it underplays the objective aspects of class. Wolfgang Abendroth's *Short History of the European Working Class* is a useful overview up to the 1970s. In addition to Trotsky's *History*, Tony Cliff's three-volume *Lenin* remains essential reading on the Russian Revolution as does Rabinowich's *The Bolsheviks Come To Power*. Daniel Kaiser's collection *The Workers' Revolution in Russia: The View from Below* contains much useful material while John Rees's et al, *In Defence of October* provides an excellent, short introduction to the debates raised. Pierre Broué's *The German Revolution* is the crucial work on an underdiscussed subject. Gabriel Kolko's *A Century of War* is a fascinating and detailed global analysis of twentieth-century warfare and class struggle, and Ian Birchall's polemical *Workers Against the Monolith* outlines some of the failings of post-war Stalinist politics. Manning Marable's *African and Caribbean Politics* comes to different conclusions from the current work but contains a mass of useful information and analysis on a range of national liberation struggles. Chris Harman's *The Fire Last Time* is an outstanding dissection of the events of 1968 and after. And the collection *Revolutionary Rehearsals in the Neoliberal Age* edited by Dale Barker and Neil Davidson is very useful for getting to grips with more recent global insurgencies.

Finally, three useful introductions to the theory and practice of revolutionary organising. *Party and Class* by Chris Harman and Tony Cliff brings together four important essays on the subject, Lukacs's *Lenin: A Study on the Unity of his Thought* is one of the best general explanations of the role of revolutionary organisation and John Rees's *Strategy and Tactics* is an invaluable guide to the application of revolutionary Marxism.

Wolfgang Abendroth (1972) *A Short History of the European Working Class,* Verso, London.

Colin Barker, Gareth Dale and Neil Davidson (2021) *Revolutionary Rehearsals in the Neoliberal Age,* Haymarket, Chicago.

Ian H. Birchall (1974) *Workers Against the Monolith,* Pluto Press, London.

Harry Braverman (1974) *Labour and Monopoly Capitalism: The Degradation of Work in the Twentieth Century,* Monthly Review Press, London.

Pierre Broué (2006) *The German Revolution 1917-1923,* Haymarket, Chicago.

Heather H. Brown (2013) *Marx on Gender and the Family,*

Haymarket, Chicago.

Tony Cliff (1975-78) *Lenin Volumes 1-3,* Bookmarks, London.

Raju Das (2017) *Marxist Class Theory for a Skeptical World,* Brill, Leiden.

Kevin Doogan (2009) *New Capitalism? The Transformation of Work,* Polity, Cambridge.

Hal Draper *Karl Marx's Theory of Revolution: The politics of Social Classes,* Monthly Review Press, New York.

Lindsey German (1996) *A Question of Class,* Bookmarks, London.

Lindsey German (2017) *Class, Wealth and Power in Neoliberal Britain,* Counterfire, London.

Lindsey German (1989) *Sex, Class and Socialism,* Bookmarks, London.

Antonio Gramsci (1971) *Selections from the Prison Notebooks,* Lawrence and Wishart, London.

Asad Haider (2018) *Mistaken Identity,* Verso, London.

Chris Harman and Tony Cliff (1997) *Party and Class,* Bookmarks, London.

Chris Harman (1998) *The Fire Last Time,* Bookmarks, London.

Daniel H Kaiser, ed, (1987) *The Workers' Revolution in Russia, 1917: The View from Below,* Cambridge University Press, Cambridge.

Gabriel Kolko (1994) *Century of War,* The New Press, New York.

Georg Lukács (1971) *History and Class Consciousness,* Merlin, London.

Georg Lukács, (2009) *Lenin, A Study in the Unity of his Thought,* Verso, London.

Rosa Luxemburg (1906) *The Mass Strike,* Bookmarks, London.

Manning Marable (1987) *African and Caribbean Politics,* Verso, London.

Karl Marx (1976) *Capital Volume 1,2* and 3, Penguin, London

Karl Marx (1871) 'The Civil War in France', in Karl Marx (1996) *Later Political Writings,* Cambridge University Press, Cambridge

Karl Marx and Friedrich Engels (2015) *The Communist Manifesto*, Penguin, London

Karl Marx (1847) 'Economic and Philosophical Manuscripts', in Karl Marx (1975) *Early Writings*, Penguin, London.

Karl Marx (1895) 'Class Struggles in France: 148-1850' in Karl Marx (1973) *Surveys From Exile*, Allen Lane, London.

Karl Marx and Friedrich Engels (1845) *The German Ideology*, Lawrence and Wishart, London.

Kim Moody (2017) *On New Terrain: How Capital Is Reshaping the Battleground of Class War*, Haymarket, Chicago.

Chris Nineham (2010) *Capitalism and Class Consciousness*, Counterfire, London.

Kevin Ovenden (1992) *Malcom X, Socialism and Black Nationalism*, Bookmarks, London.

Alexander Rabinowitch (2017) *The Bolsheviks Come to Power: The Revolution of 1917 in Petrograd*, Haymarket Books, Chicago.

John Rees, Robert W. Service, Sam Farber, Robin Blackburn (1997) *In Defence of October: A debate on the Russian Revolution*, London, Bookmarks.

John Rees (2010) *Strategy and Tactics, How the Left can Organise to Transform Society*, Counterfire, London.

John Rees (1998) *The Algebra of Revolution*, Routledge, London.

Beverly J. Silver (2003) *Forces of Labor: Worker's Movements and Globalization since 1870*, Cambridge University Press, New York.

Keeanga-Yamahtta Taylor (2016) *From #BlackLivesMatter to Black Liberation*, Haymarket, Chicago.

E.P. Thompson (2013) *The Making of the English Working Class*, Verso, London.

Endnotes

1   Antonio Labriola (1966) *Essays on the Materialist Conception of History*, Monthly Review Press, New York, p.155.

2   George Orwell, (2001) *The Road to Wigan Pier*, introduction, Richard Hoggart, Penguin, London, p.15.

3   Rosa Luxemburg (1918) 'Our Program and the Political Situation', in Rosa Luxemburg (1971) *Selected Political Writings*, Monthly Review Press, London, p.72.

4   'Leader's speech, Bournemouth 1999, Tony Blair, Labour', *British Political Speech Archive*, Available at: http://www.briti shpoliticalspeech.org/speech-archive.htm?speech=205

5   See for example, Arun Kundnani (2020) 'What is racial capitalism?' Text of a talk by Arun Kundnani at the Havens Wright Center for Social Justice, University of Wisconsin-Madison, October 15, 2020. Available at: https://www. kundnani.org/what-is-racial-capitalism/

6   See Lindsey German (1996) *A Question of Class,* Bookmarks, London, p.31.

7   See for example, Patrick Butler (June 29, 2016) 'Most Britons regard themselves as working class, survey finds', *The Guardian,* available at: https://www.theguardian.com/ society/2016/jun/29/most-brits-regard-themselves-as-working-class-survey-finds

8   Robert Bird and Frank Newport (February 27, 2017) 'What Determines How Americans Perceive Their Social Class?', *Gallup,* available at: https://news.gallup.com/opinion/ polling-matters/204497/deter mines-americans-perceive-social-class.aspx

9   For a discussion of the data about working-class opinion see Chris Nineham (2017) *How the Establishment Lost Control,* Zero, Hants, pp.22-3.

10 Karl Marx and Friedrich Engels (2015) *The Communist*

Manifesto, Penguin, London, p.6.

11   International Labour Organisation (2013) 'Key Indicators of the Labour Market', 8th ed. ILO, Geneva, available at: https://www.ilo.org/wcmsp5/groups/public/---dgreports/---stat/documents/publication/wcms_498929.pdf

12   The World Labor Group (WLG) database is one of the empirical sources used in this book to understand patterns of labour unrest. This database originates in a collective research effort by a group of graduate students and faculty (The World Labor Research Working Group) at the Fernand Braudel Center (Binghamton University) in the 1980s. The findings and methods of the database are discussed in Beverly J. Silver (2003) *Forces of Labor: Worker's Movements and Globalization since 1870,* Cambridge University Press, New York, see particularly Appendix A, pp.181-98.

13   There is widespread evidence of a sharp increase in protest globally over the last few decades. See for example, Pippa Norris (2003) *Democratic Phoenix: Reinventing Political Activism*, Cambridge University Press, Massachusetts. See also D.J. Bailey (11 January, 2016) 'Hard Evidence: This is the Age of Dissent and there is much more to come', *The Conversation*. Available at: https://theconversation.com/hard-evidence-this-is-the-age-of-dissent-and-theres-much-more-to-come-52871 and Ady Cousins (November 27, 2011) 'The Crisis of the British Regime: Democracy, Protest and the Unions', *Counterfire.* Available at: https://www.counterfire.org/theory/37-theory/14906-the-crisis-of-the-british-regime-democracy-protest-and-the-unions

14   See for example, (February 23, 2016) 'Socialism more popular with British people than capitalism, survey finds' *The Independent*. Available at: https://www.independent.co.uk/news/uk/politics/socialism-is-more-popular-with-the-british-public-than-capitalism-survey-finds-a6892371.html For a summary of polling in the UK and the US showing sharp

rises in support for socialism in both countries see, Owen Jones (September 20, 2021) 'Eat the rich! Why millennials and generation Z have turned their backs on capitalism', *The Guardian*. Available at: https://www.theguardian.com/ politics/2021/sep/20/eat-the-rich-why-millennials-and-generation-z-have-turned-their-backs-on-capitalism

15 See for example, Ian Kullgren, Brian Eckhouse and Deena Shanker (October 17,2021) 'US Labor Unions Are Having a Moment', *Time Magazine*. Available at: https://time. com/6107676/labor-unions/

Also, Dominic Bernard (January 12, 2022) 'Strikes return after pandemic reprieve', *HR Magazine*. Available at: https:// www.hrmagazine.co.uk/content/news/strikes-return-after-pandemic-reprieve

16 See for example, Beverly J. Silver (2003) *Forces of Labor: Workers' Movements and Globalization since 1870,* Cambridge University Press, New York, and Leopold H. Haimson and Charles Tilly, eds, (2002) *Strikes, Wars, and Revolutions in an International Perspective: Strike Waves in the Late Nineteenth and Early Twentieth Centuries,* Cambridge University Press, New York.

17 Friedrich Nietzsche, 'On Truth and Lies in the Nonmoral Sense', in Walter Kaufmann, ed, (1954) *The Portable Nietzsche,* Viking Press, New York, p.45.

For a useful discussion of the impact of 1848 on the intellectual world see Georg Lukács (1989) *The Historical Novel,* Merlin, London, pp.171 and ff.

18 See Goran Therborn (1976) *Science, Class and Society,* Verso, London, especially pp.424-9.

19 Georg Lukács (1971) *History and Class Consciousness*, Merlin, London, p.66.

20 'Karl Marx to J. Weydemeyer in New York', 5 March 1852, London, *Marxist Internet Archive* available here: https://www.marxists.org/archive/marx/works/1852/

letters/52_03_05-ab.htm

21 *Poor Man's Guardian*, 19 October 1833: Quoted in E.P.
    Thompson (1980) *The Making of the English Working Class*,
    Penguin, London, p.833.

22 Karl Marx and Friedrich Engels (1856) *The Holy Family. or
    Critique of Critical Criticism, Against Bruno Bauer and Company*,
    Foreign Languages Publishing House, Moscow, p.52.

23 Karl Marx and Freidrich Engels (1970) *The German Ideology*,
    Lawrence and Wishart, London, p.47.

24 Karl Marx (1859) 'Preface to a Contribution to the Critique
    of Political Economy', in Karl Marx (1975) *Early Writings*,
    Penguin, London, p.425.

25 Karl Marx (1847) 'Economic and Philosophical Manuscripts',
    in Karl Marx (1975) *Early Writings*, Penguin, London, p.345.

26 Marx writes about Guizot's development in his essay
    England's 'Seventeenth Century Revolution' https://
    www.marxists.org/archive/marx/works/1850/02/english-
    revolution.htm

27 Max Weber (2017) *General Economic History First Edition*,
    Routledge, London, p.79. Weber was here summarising
    Marx's argument in Karl Marx (1976) *Capital Volume 1*,
    Penguin, London, pp.344-52.

28 Karl Marx (1973) *Grundrisse*, Penguin, London, p.106.

29 Karl Marx and Friedrich Engels (2015) *The Communist
    Manifesto*, Penguin, London, p.2.

30 Karl Marx (1973) *Grundrisse*, Penguin, London, p.100.

31 Karl Marx and Friedrich Engels (1970) *The German Ideology*,
    Lawrence and Wishart, London, p.46.

32 Karl Marx and Freidrich Engels (1970) *The German Ideology*,
    Lawrence and Wishart, London, p.47.

33 Karl Marx (1987) *Theories of Surplus Value*, Lawrence and
    Wishart, London. p.399.

34 Karl Marx (1976) *Capital Volume 1*, Penguin, London, p.508.

35 Karl Marx (1844) 'Economic and Philosophical Manuscripts',

in Karl Marx (1975) *Early Writings,* Penguin, London, p.324.

36   Karl Marx (1976) *Capital Volume 1*, Penguin, London, p.548.

37   Karl Marx (1955) *Poverty of Philosophy*, Progress, Moscow, p.22.

38   Karl Marx (1976) *Capital Volume 1*, Penguin, London, p.509.

39   Karl Marx (1973) *Grundrisse*, Penguin, London, p.95.

40   For an in-depth discussion of these points see Terrell Carver, ed, (1975) *Karl Marx: Texts on Method,* Oxford: Blackwell, p.109-29.

41   'Just 8 Men Own Same Wealth as Half the World', Oxfam Report January 15, 2017, available at: https://www.oxfamamerica.org/press/just-8-men-own-same-wealth-as-half-the-world/

42   Karl Marx (1955) *Poverty of Philosophy*, Progress, Moscow, p.80.

43   Karl Marx (1955) *Poverty of Philosophy*, Progress, Moscow, p.79.

44   Karl Marx and Friedrich Engels (2015) *The Communist Manifesto*, Penguin, London, p.19.

45   Karl Marx (1844) 'Introduction to Hegel's Philosophy of Right', in Karl Marx (1975) *Early Writings,* Penguin, London, p.256.

46   Karl Marx and Friedrich Engels (1856) *The Holy Family or Critique of Critical Criticism, Against Bruno Bauer and Company*, Foreign Languages Publishing House, Moscow, p.52.

47   Karl Marx (1844) 'Introduction to Hegel's Philosophy of Right', in Karl Marx (1975) *Early Writings,* Penguin, London, p.256.

48   Friedrich Engels (1978) *The Origin of the Family, Private Property and the State,* Foreign Languages Press, Peking, p.75.

49   Karl Marx (1845) 'Peuchet on Suicide', *Marxist Internet Archive*, available at: https://marxists.architexturez.net/archive/marx/works /1845/09/suicide.htm

50   Karl Marx (1976) *Capital Volume 1*, Penguin, London, p.621.

For wider discussions of Marx's approach to women's oppression see, amongst others, Lindsey German (1989) *Sex, Class and Socialism,* Bookmarks, London. Also Heather H. Brown (2013) *Marx on Gender and the Family,* Chicago, Haymarket.

51   'Marx to Sigfrid Meyer and August Vogt In New York', in Karl Marx and Friedrich Engels (1975) *Selected Correspondence,* Progress Publishers, Moscow, pp. 220-29.

52   Karl Marx (1976) *Capital Volume 1,* Penguin, London, p.329.

53   'Marx to Sigfrid Meyer and August Vogt in New York', in Karl Marx and Friedrich Engels (1975) *Selected Correspondence,* Progress Publishers, Moscow, p.220.

54   Friedrich Engels (1872) 'Meeting in Hyde Park', in Karl Marx and Friedrich Engels (1971) *Marx and Engels on Ireland,* Progress Publishers, Moscow, p.26.

55   Karl Marx (1845) 'Theses on Feuerbach', in Karl Marx and Friedrich Engels (1970) *The German Ideology,* Lawrence and Wishart, London, p.121.

56   Karl Marx and Friedrich Engels (1970) *The German Ideology,* Lawrence and Wishart, London, p.64.

57   Karl Marx and Friedrich Engels (1970) *The German Ideology,* Lawrence and Wishart, London, p.47.

58   Karl Marx (1973) *Grundrisse,* Penguin, London, p.251.

59   Karl Marx and Friedrich Engels (2015) *The Communist Manifesto,* Penguin, London, p.14.

60   Friedrich Engels (1975) *Ludwig Feuerbach and the End of Classical German Philosophy,* Progress Publishers, Moscow, p.2.

61   Karl Marx (1845) 'Theses on Feuerbach', In Karl Marx and Friedrich Engels (1970) *The German Ideology,* Lawrence and Wishart, London, p.95.

62   Karl Marx (1864) 'Inaugural Address of the International Workingmen's Association', in Karl Marx (1974) *The First International and After,* Penguin, London, p.78.

63   Friedrich Engels (2009) *The Condition of the Working Class in England*, Penguin, London, p.84.

64   Karl Marx and Friedrich Engels (1845) *The German Ideology*, Lawrence and Wishart, London, pp.204–5.

65   Karl Marx (1969) *Value, Price and Profit*, International Co., Inc, New York, p.32.

66   Karl Marx (1852) The Eighteenth Brumaire of Louis Bonaparte in Karl Marx (1973) *Surveys from Exile*, Penguin, London, pp.210-211.

67   Karl Marx, (1874) 'The English Elections', in Karl Marx and Friedrich Engels (1955) *On Britain,* Progress, Moscow, p.64.

68   Karl Marx (1875) 'Critique of the Gotha Programme', in Karl Marx (1973) *The First International and After*, Penguin, London, p.353.

69   Friedrich Engels (1888) 'Preface to the English Edition of the Communist Manifesto', in Marx and Engels (1984) *Basic Writings on Politics and Philosophy*, Fontana, Aylesbury, p.46.

70   Karl Marx (1843) 'Letter to Ruge', in Karl Marx (1973) *Early Writings*, Penguin, London, p.206.

71   Karl Marx (1871) 'The Civil War in France', in Karl Marx (1996) *Later Political Writings*, Cambridge University Press, Cambridge, p.189.

72   Jürgen Kocka (1986) 'Problems of Working-Class Formation in Germany: The Early Years, 1800-1875', in Ira Katznelson and Aristide R. Zolberg, eds, (1986) *Working-Class Formation, Nineteenth-Century Patterns in Western Europe and the United States*, Princeton University Press, Princeton, pp.296-7.

73   Beverly J. Silver (2003) *Forces of Labor: Workers' Movements and Globalization Since 1870,* Cambridge University Press, New York, p.135.

74   Julius Braunthal (1966) *History of the International,* Volume 1, Praeger/Gollancz, London pp.196-7.

75   Electoral figures from Duncan Hallas (1985) *The Comintern,* Bookmarks, London, pp.14-15.

76 Wolfgang Abendroth (1972) *A Short History of the European Working Class,* Verso, London, pp.56-7.

77 Karl Bernstein (2012) *Preconditions of Socialism,* Cambridge University Press, Cambridge, p.208.

78 Karl Kautsky (1971) *The Class Struggle: Erfurt Programme,* W.W. Norton, New York, p.200.

79 Rosa Luxemburg (1986) *Social Reform or Revolution,* Militant, London, p.24.

80 Vladimir Lenin (1904) 'One Step Forward Two Steps Back', In Vladimir Lenin (1942) *Selected Works, Volume 2,* Lawrence and Wishart, London, p.407.

81 Vladimir Ilyich Lenin (1942) *The Two Tactics of Social Democracy,* Lawrence and Wishart, London, p.1.

82 Beverly J. Silver (2003) *Forces of Labor: Workers' Movements and Globalization since 1870,* Cambridge University Press, New York, figure 4.2, p.132.

83 A.J.P. Taylor (1954) *The Struggle for Mastery in Europe 1848-1918,* Oxford University Press, London, p.529.

84 See, Beverly J. Silver (2003) *Forces of Labor: Workers' Movements and Globalization Since 1870,* Cambridge University Press, New York, p.157, and Douglas A. Hibbs Jr. (1978) 'On the Political Economy of Long-Run Trends in Strike Activity', *British Journal of Political Science* 8:(2), April, 153-75 (1978), p.157.

85 Pierre Broué (2006) *The German Revolution 1917-1923,* Haymarket, Chicago, p.151.

86 Wolfgang Abendroth (1972) *A Short History of the European Working Class,* Verso, London, pp.70-1.

87 Quoted in Julius Braunthal (1967) *History of the International, Volume 2,* Frederick A. Praeger, New York, pp.168-9.

88 Steve A. Smith (1987) 'Petrograd in 1917, The View from Below', in Daniel H Kaiser, ed, (1987) *The Workers' Revolution in Russia, 1917: The View from Below,* Cambridge University Press, Cambridge, p.78.

89   N.N. Sukhanov (2014) *The Russian Revolution 1917: A Personal Record,* Princeton Legacy Library, Princeton, p.308.

90   The official statement of support for the seizure of power issued by the All Russian Conference of Factory-Shop Committees is a wonderfully measured and sober recognition of this fact:

'The working-class has much more interest in the proper and uninterrupted operation of the factories...than the capitalist class. Workers' control is a better security in this respect for the interests of modern society, of the whole people, than the arbitrary will of the owners who are guided only by their selfish desire for material profits or political privileges. Therefore workers' control is demanded by the proletariat not only in their own interest, but in the interests of the whole country, and should be supported by the revolutionary peasantry as well as the revolutionary army.'

Quoted in John Reed (2007) *Ten Days That Shook the World,* Penguin, London, p.295.

91   Morgan Phillips Price (1997) *Dispatches from the Revolution, Russia 1916-18,* Pluto, London, p.92.

92   Quoted in Tony Cliff (1989) *Trotsky: Towards October 1879-1917,* Bookmarks, London, p.286.

93   Quoted in Paolo Spriano (1975) *The Occupation of the Factories,* Pluto, London, p.132.

94   Pierre Broué (2006) *The German Revolution 1917-1923,* Haymarket, Chicago, pp.157-8.

95   Pierre Broué (2006) *The German Revolution 1917-1923,* Haymarket, Chicago, p.158.

96   Pierre Broué (2006) *The German Revolution 1917-1923,* Haymarket, Chicago, p.152.

97   Quoted in Paolo Spriano (1964) *The Occupation of the Factories, Italy, 1920,* Pluto, London, p.90.

98   The classic analysis of the transformation of the post-revolutionary soviet into Stalinist state capitalism remains

Tony Cliff (1996) *State Capitalism in Russia,* Bookmarks, London.

99   Leon Trotsky (2008) *History of the Russian Revolution,* Haymarket, Chicago, p.1101

100   Leon Trotsky (2008) *History of the Russian Revolution,* Haymarket, Chicago, p.17.

101   Leon Trotsky (2008) *History of the Russian Revolution,* Haymarket, Chicago, p.1.

102   Leon Trotsky (1971) *The Struggle against Fascism in Germany,* Pathfinder, London, p.139.

103   Leon Trotsky (1971) *The Struggle against Fascism in Germany,* Pathfinder, London, p.194.

104   Leon Trotsky (1971) *The Struggle against Fascism in Germany,* Pathfinder, London, pp.194-5.

105   Antonio Gramsci (1971) *Selections from the Prison Notebooks,* Lawrence and Wishart, London, p.333.

106   Antonio Gramsci (1971) *Selections from the Prison Notebooks,* Lawrence and Wishart, London, p.12.

107   Antonio Gramsci (1971) *Selections from the Prison Notebooks,* Lawrence and Wishart, London p.80.

108   Antonio Gramsci (1971) *Selections from the Prison Notebooks,* Lawrence and Wishart, London, p.330. Marx's letter to Ruge is quoted above on p.30.

109   For a discussion of the (false) attribution of this phrase and idea to Gramsci, see Joseph A. Buttigieg (1995) 'Gramsci on Civil Society', *Boundary 2,* Volume 22, No. 3 (Autumn), pp.1-32. For evidence that Gramsci embraced the Bolsheviks' policy of the united front and that in general he was moving towards rather than diverging from Leninism in the mid-1920s, see Antonio Gramsci (2014) *A Great and Terrible World: The Pre-Prison Letters 1908-1926,* Lawrence and Wishart, London.

110   Antonio Gramsci, 'The Southern Question', in Gramsci (1957) *The Modern Prince and Other Writings,* Lawrence and Wishart,

London, p.30.

111 For an indepth discussion of the relationship between Gramsci's and Lukács' ideas on consciousness, see John Rees (1998) *The Algebra of Revolution*, Routledge, London, pp.202-52.

112 Georg Lukács (1971) *History and Class Consciousness*, Merlin, London, p.89.

113 Quoted in John Rees (1998) *The Algebra of Revolution*, Routledge, London, p.72.

114 Georg Lukács (1971) *History and Class Consciousness*, Merlin, London p.169.

115 Georg Lukács (1971), p.21.

116 Georg Lukács (1971) *History and Class Consciousness*, Merlin, London p.310.

117 Anthony Crossland (2006) *The Future of Socialism*, Constable, London, p.115.

118 Anthony Crossland (2006) *The Future of Socialism*, Constable, London, p.62.

119 Parsons essay 'An analytical Approach to the Theory of Stratification' appeared in 1940 and is included in Talcott Parsons (1964) *Essays in Sociological Theory*, Free Press, New York, pp.69-88. See also Goran Therborn (1980) *Science, Class and Society,* Verso, London pp.422-9, for a useful discussion of post-classical period sociology.

120 Daniel Bell (2000) *The End of Ideology*, Harvard University Press, Cambridge, p.84.

121 Quoted in Ian H. Birchall (1974) *Workers Against the Monolith,* Pluto Press, London, p.84.

122 Ian H. Birchall (1974) *Workers Against the Monolith,* Pluto Press, London, p.89.

123 John Strachey (1956) *Contemporary Capitalism*, London, Gollancz, p.235.

124 Michel Aglietta (1979) *A Theory of Capitalist Regulation*, New Left Books, London, p.165.

125 Gerard Dumenil and Dominique Levy (2004) *Capital Resurgent: Roots of the Neoliberal Revolution,* Harvard University Press, Cambridge.

126 David Harvey (2007) *A Brief History of Neoliberalism,* Oxford University Press, Oxford, p.10.

127 Winston S. Churchill (1960) *The Second World War Volume 1, The Gathering Storm,* Penguin, London, p.198.

128 Gabriel Kolko (1994) *Century of War,* The New Press, New York, pp.281.

129 Gabriel Kolko (1994) *Century of War,* The New Press, New York, pp.282-3.

130 Caroline Moorhead (2019) *A House in the Mountains: The Women Who Liberated Italy from Fascism,* Chatto and Windus, London, p.312.

131 Gabriel Kolko (1994) *Century of War,* The New Press, New York, p.253. In Kolko's opinion: 'In many regards these strike movements were far more visible and politically significant in their impact on the masses than the partisan activities.'

132 Ian H. Birchall (1974) *Workers Against the Monolith,* Pluto Press, London, p.30.
The Italian Communist Party membership figures are from Kolko (1994), *Century of War,* The New Press, New York, p.291.

133 Caroline Moorhead (2019) *A House in the Mountains: The Women Who Liberated Italy from Fascism,* Chatto and Windus, London, p.312.

134 Quoted in Kolko (1994) *Century of War,* The New Press, New York, p.278.

135 Zygmunt Zaremba (1997) *The Warsaw Commune: Betrayed by Stalin, Massacred by Hitler,* Socialist Platform, London, pp.39-40.

136 Economist (October 7, 1944), quoted in Ygael Gluckstein (1952) *Stalin's Satellites in Eastern Europe,* Allen and Unwin, London, pp.132-3.

137 See Raquel Varela (2021) *A People's History of Europe*, London, Pluto, p.92.

138 Paul Addison (1985) *Now The War Is Over: A Social History of Britain 1945-51*, BBC and Jonathan Cape, London, p.55.

139 Quoted in Geoffrey Lewis (2002) 'Quintin McGarel Hogg, Lord Hailsham of St Marylebone, 9 October 1907 – 12 October 2001', in *Biographical Memoirs of Fellows of the Royal Society*, Royal Society publishing, available at: https://royalsocietypublishing.org/doi/ 10.1098/rsbm.2002.0012

140 The document announcing the dissolution of the Communist International in 1943 spells this out: '...in the countries of the Hitlerite bloc the basic task of the workers, toilers and all honest people is to contribute in every conceivable way towards the defeat of this bloc by undermining the Hitlerite war machine from within, by helping to overthrow the governments responsible for the war, in the countries of the anti-Hitler coalition the sacred duty of the broadest masses of the people, and first and foremost of progressive workers, is to support in every way the war efforts of the governments of those countries for the sake of the speediest destruction of the Hitlerite bloc and to secure friendly collaboration between the nations on the basis of their equal rights.' Document quoted in Fridrikh Igorevich Firsov, Harvey Klehr and John Earl Haynes (2014) *Secret Cables of the Comintern, 1933-1943*, New Haven: Yale University Press, p.243.

141 Quoted in Gabriel Kolko (1994) *Century of War*, The New Press, New York, p.297.

142 The mass of French communists was shaken by this blow and across the country they refused to give up the weapons that they had used during the Liberation, preferring to hide them under floors or in gardens. After one such cache was found by the gendamerie at Valencennes, former members of the FTP threatened to attack the local police station if there were any more searches. See Anthony Beevor and Artemis Cooper

(1994) *Paris After the Liberation*, Penguin, London, p.111.

143 Taken from a speech to miners at Waziers in July 1945, quoted in Ian Birchall (1974) *Workers Against the Monolith. The Communist Parties since 1943*, Pluto, London, p.29.

144 Gabriel Kolko (1994) *Century of War*, The New Press, New York, p.294.

145 Gabriel Kolko (1994) *Century of War*, The New Press, New York, p.297.

146 Ian Birchall (1974) *Workers Against the Monolith. The Communist Parties Since 1943*, Pluto, London, p.31.

147 C Harman (2009) *Zombie Capitalism: Global Crisis and the Relevance of Marx*, London, Bookmarks, p.161.

148 Rather than the boom being a product of a class compromise on wages or welfarism and state intervention and a resulting increase in consumption, the process actually took place the other way around. The initial exit from crisis at the end of the 1930s was marked by a sharp rise in the rate of profit. There is no way that growth in consumption can explain such dramatic movements in this fundamental economic variable, but it was this high rate of profit which explains the continuously high level of investment by capitalists throughout the period.

The most coherent explanation for the increase in the rate of profit lies not in the suppression of capitalism's fundamental contradictions, but actually in its irrationalities, particularly its tendency towards military competition. The slump of the 1930s and the war that followed meant that vast amounts of capital had been written off. Shane Mage, for instance, calculates that the amount of capital held by US firms shrank by 20 per cent between 1930 and 1945. This encouraged a new round of capital accumulation. The continued military competition of the Cold War meant that vast amounts of investment which would otherwise have raised the ratio of investment to labour were used for military purposes. Michael

Kidron explained the dynamic by which a 'permanent arms economy' thus had the effect of slowing down the long-term tendency of the rate of profit to fall. It was not, Kidron argued, that 'an arms budget was ever adopted anywhere as a means of securing an international environment conducive to stability', but 'the important point is that the very existence of national military machines of the current size, however happened upon, both increases the chance of economic stability and compels other nation states to adopt a definite type of response and behaviour, which requires no policing by some overall authority.' Michael Kidron (1967) 'A Permanent Arms Economy', in Michael Kidron and Richard Kuper (2018) *Capitalism and Theory: Selected Writings of Michael Kidron*, Haymarket Books, Chicago, p.123.

149   These figures are from Gerard Dumenil, Mark Glick and Jose Rangel (1987) 'The Rate of Profit in the United States', *Cambridge Journal of Economics*, Oxford University Press, vol. 11(4), pp.351-3. In his book *Zombie Capitalism*, Chris Harman summarises 'various interpretations of the rate of profit in these decades', by saying, 'different ways of measuring are used, and the figures differ somewhat from each other, with some showing a long-term decline and some a dip in the mid-1950s. But none of them show a fall to the level of the first three decades of the Twentieth Century, or to the level of the late 1970s'; Chris Harman (2009), p.371.

150   Meghnad Desai (1981) *Testing Monetarism,* Frances Pinter, London, p.101.

151   Robert Brenner (2006) *The Economics of Global Turbulence: The Advanced Capitalist Economies from Long Boom to Long Downturn, 1945-2005*, Verso, London, p.94.

152   Michel Aglietta (2015) *A Theory of Capitalist Regulation, The US Experience,* Verso, London, p.194.

153   Gerard Dumenil, Mark Glick and Jose Rangel (1987), 'The Rate of Profit in the United States', *Cambridge Journal of*

Economics, Oxford University Press, vol. 11(4), p.339.

154 Robert Brenner and Mark Glick (1991) 'The Regulation Approach: Theory and History', *New Left Review* 188.1 (July/August).

155 Figures from Harry Braverman (1974) *Labour and Monopoly Capitalism: The Degradation of Work in the Twentieth Century,* Monthly Review Press, London, p.262.

156 Chris Harman (1998) *The Fire Last Time,* Bookmarks, London, p.16.

157 Harry Braverman (1974) *Labour and Monopoly Capitalism: The Degradation of Work in the Twentieth Century,* Monthly Review Press, London, p.307.

158 Figures from Harry Braverman (1974) *Labour and Monopoly Capitalism: The Degradation of Work in the Twentieth Century,* Monthly Review Press, London, p.204.

159 'A Guide to Office Clerical Time Standards: A Compilation of Standard Data Used by Large American Companies' (Detroit, 1960). Quoted in Harry Braverman (1974), p.221.

160 For fascinating interviews with the activists who started the movement, see the documentary film *9 to 5: The Story of a Movement* (2020) AFI Docs, June 2020, Produced by Julia Reichert and Steven Bognar.

161 Barbara and John Ehrenreich, 'The Professional and Managerial Class', in Pat Walker, ed, (1979) *Between Labour and Capital,* Hassocks: Harvester Press, p.18.
For a further discussion of the Ehrenreichs' thesis, see Lindsey German (1996) *A Question of Class*, Bookmarks, London, p.69.

162 In the US, for example, the number of stoppages increased from 3333 in 1960 to 4700 in 1968. More dramatically, 'Man-hours lost' (sic) rose from 19,100,000 to 42,390,000. Figures from the US Department of Labour's Monthly Labor Review April 1969, quoted in Kim Moody, 'The American Working Class in Transition', *International Socialism* (First Series) October/November 1969, p.11.

163 Colin Barker, 'Striking Statistics', *International Socialism* (1st series), February 1973, pp.12-14.

164 Allan Flanders (1980) 'Collective Bargaining: Prescription of No Change', in A. Flanders (1980) *Management and the Unions: The Theory and Reform of Industrial Relations*, Faber, London, p.169.

165 Lord Donovan (1971) *Royal Commission on Trade Unions and Employers' Associations 1965-1968*, Her Majesty's Stationary Office, London, p.43.

166 Tony Cliff (2002) *In the Thick of Workers' Struggle: Selected Works, Volume 2*, Bookmarks, London, pp.129–43.

167 See for example Everett M. Kassalow (1963) *National Labor Movements in the Postwar World*, Northwestern University, Chicago.

168 The British Viceroy and Governor-General of India, Lord Wavell, advised Churchill that 'the repressive force necessary to hold India after the war would exceed Britain's means'. See Brian Lapping (1985) *End of Empire*, Paladin, London, p.356.

169 John Iliffe (1975) 'The Creation of Group Consciousness Among the Dockworkers of Dar es Salaam, 1929-1950', in Richard Sandbrook and Robin Cohen, eds, (1975) *The Development of an African Working Class: Studies in Class Formation and Action*, Longman, Toronto, pp.49-72.

170 C.L.R. James (1977) *Nkrumah and the Ghana Revolution*, Allison and Busby, London, p.133.

171 Manning Marable (1987) *African and Caribbean Politics*, Verso, London, p.55.

172 Jafar Suryomenggolo (2011) 'Workers' Control in Java, Indonesia, 1945-1946', in Immanuel Ness and Dario Azzellini (2011) *Ours to Master and to Own: Workers' Control from the Commune to the Present*, Chicago, Haymarket Books, p.216.

173 Quoted in Ian Clegg (1971) *Workers Self-Management in Algeria*, Allen Lane, London p.49.

174 Jafar Suryomenggolo (2011) 'Workers' Control in Java, Indonesia, 1945-1946', in Immanuel Ness and Dario Azzellini (2011) *Ours to Master and to Own: Workers' Control from the Commune to the Present*, Chicago, Haymarket Books, pp.222-5.

175 Samuel J Southgate (2011) 'From Workers' Self-Management to State Bureuacratic Control: Autogestion in Algeria', in Immanuel Ness and Dario Azzellini (2011) *Ours to Master and to Own: Workers' Control from the Commune to the Present*, Chicago, Haymarket Books, pp.233-7.

176 Samuel J. Southgate (2011) 'From Workers' Self-Management to State Bureuacratic Control: Autogestion in Algeria', in Immanuel Ness and Dario Azzellini (2011) *Ours to Master and to Own: Workers' Control from the Commune to the Present*, Chicago, Haymarket Books, p.245.

177 Jafar Suryomenggolo (2011) 'Workers' Control in Java, Indonesia, 1945-1946', in Immanuel Ness and Dario Azzellini (2011) *Ours to Master and to Own: Workers' Control from the Commune to the Present*, Chicago, Haymarket Books, p.212.

178 See Tony Cliff (1963) *Deflected Permanent Revolution*, Socialist Workers Party, London, p.20.

179 Manning Marable (1987) *African and Caribbean Politics*, Verso, London, pp.49-51.

180 Samuel Southgate (2011) 'From Workers' Self-Management to State Bureaucratic Control: Autogestion in Algeria', in Immanuel Ness and Dario Azzellini (2011) *Ours to Master and to Own: Workers' Control from the Commune to the Present*, Chicago, Haymarket Books, p.246.

181 C. A. Mayers (1959) 'India', in Walter Galenson, ed, (1959) *Labor and Economic Development*, John Wiley, New York, pp.41-2.

182 V.B. Karnick (1960) *Indian Trade Unionism: A Survey,* Labour Education Service, Bombay, pp.227-228.

183 Quoted in Ian Birchall (1974) *Workers Against the Monolith.*

The Communist Parties Since 1943, Pluto, London, p.54.

184 Irene Norlund (2004) 'Trade unions in Vietnam in Historical Perspective', in Rebecca Elamhurst and Ratna Saptari, eds, (2004) *Labour in South East Asia: Local Processes in a Globalised World*, Routledge, London, p.108.

185 Quoted in Manning Marable (1987) *African and Caribbean Politics*, Verso, London, p.150.

186 Figures from Chris Harman (1998) *The Fire Last Time*, Bookmarks, London, p.39.

187 Student leader Mario Savio from Berkeley California, who had been involved in the civil-rights Freedom Summer in Mississippi in 1964, expressed the mood of emerging movement brilliantly:
'The most exciting things going on in America today are the movements to change America. America is becoming ever more the utopia of sterilised, automated contentment...This chrome plated consumers' paradise would have us grow up to be well-behaved children. But an important minority of men and women...have shown they would rather die than be standardised, replaceable and irrelevant.'
Quoted in Hal Draper (1965) *Berkeley; The New Student Revolt*, New York, p.182.

188 *The Report of the President's Commission on Campus Unrest* (1970) Washington D.C. Government Printing Office, pp.18, 39, 48. Quoted in Maurice Isserman and Michael Kazin (2000) *America Divided: The Civil War of the 1960s*, Oxford University Press, Oxford, p.268.

189 SDS's call for the demonstration showed how barbarity in Vietnam was further radicalising the movement:
'We are outraged that $2 million dollars a day is expended for war on the poor in Vietnam, while government financing is so desperately needed to abolish poverty at home. What kind of America is it whose response to poverty and oppression in Vietnam is napalm and defoliation? Whose response to

poverty and oppression in Mississippi is silence?' Quoted in Fred Halstead (1991) *Out Now! A participant's account of the movement in the US against the Vietnam War,* Pathfinder, New York, p.35.

190 Most of these examples come from the fascinating survey of the international movement in Chris Dixon and Jon Piccini (2018) 'The Anti-Vietnam War Movement: International activism and the search for world peace', in Christian Philip Peterson, William M. Knoblauch and Michael Loadenthal, eds. (2018) *The Routledge History of World Peace Since 1750,* Routledge London, pp.371-81.

191 Nanni Balestrini (2016) *We Want Everything,* London, Verso, p.68.

192 Lord Donovan (1971) *Royal Commission on Trade Unions and Employers' Associations 1965-1968,* Her Majesty's Stationary Office, London, paras 70-1.

193 Ian Birchall (1987) 'France 1968: "All power to the imagination!"' in Colin Barker, ed, (1987) *Revolutionary Rehearsals,* Bookmarks, London, p.24.

194 The dynamics of this process in Britain was well analysed in Tony Cliff (1969) 'On Perspectives', in *International Socialism* (1st series), No.36, April–May 1969, pp. 15–21.

195 For a useful account of the Portuguese revolutionary process, see Peter Robinson (1987) 'Portugal 174-75: Popular Power', in Colin Barker, ed. (1987) *Revolutionary Rehearsals,* Bookmarks, London, pp.83-122.

196 André Gorz (1968) 'Reform or revolution', in *Socialist Register,* Volume 5, Monthly Review Press, New York, p.111.

197 Tony Cliff (1969) 'On Perspectives', *International Socialism* (1st series), No.36, April–May 1969, pp.16. Cliff goes on to make the important point that the new situation which develops dialectically out of the interaction between sectional working-class confidence and political confrontation doesn't automatically overcome the weaknesses of the previous

period, elements of which continue in the new.

198 Ernest Mandel (1968) 'The Lessons of May 1968', in *New Left Review* I/52, November–December 1968, (Special Issue on France May 1968).

199 Ian Birchall (1987) 'France 1968: "All power to the imagination!"' in Colin Barker, ed, (1987) *Revolutionary Rehearsals,* Bookmarks, London, pp.21-2.

200 Ian Birchall (1987), p.21.

201 Polls in the mid-1970s consistently found that almost two-thirds of Britons believed there to be 'a class struggle in this country', double the level recorded at the start of the decade. See Jon Lawrence and Florence Sutcliffe-Braithwaite (2012) 'Margaret Thatcher and the decline of class politics', in Ben Jackson, Robert Saunders (2012) *Making Thatcher's Britain,* Cambridge University Press, Cambridge, p.133.

202 Peregrine Worsthorne, quoted in Ellen Meiksins Wood (1986) *The Retreat from Class, A New 'True' Socialism,* Verso, New York, p.182.

203 Jon Lawrence and Florence Sutcliffe-Braithwaite (2012), 'Margaret Thatcher and the decline of class politics', in Ben Jackson, Robert Saunders (2012) *Making Thatcher's Britain,* Cambridge University Press, Cambridge, p.132.

204 Margaret Thatcher (1992) 'Don't Undo My Work: No Such Thing as Majorism', *Margaret Thatcher Archive*, April 27. Originally published in Newsweek. http://www.margaretthatcher.org/document/111359.

205 Jon Lawrence and Florence Sutcliffe-Braithwaite (2012) 'Margaret Thatcher and the decline of class politics', in Ben Jackson, Robert Saunders (2012) *Making Thatcher's Britain,* Cambridge University Press, Cambridge, p.134.

206 Quoted in Mike Davis (1986) *Prisoners of the American Dream,* Verso, London, p.175.

207 When the onset of economic crisis in the 1970s revealed that a semi-Keynesian mixed economy was after all not the

secret to overcoming capitalism's contradictions, Labour and Democrat governments responded by attacking the working class and the poor. This eroded their support, undermined any possibility that they could lead opposition to the right's onslaught and, worst of all, legitimised the idea that there was no alternative to balanced budgets, austerity and free-market economics in general. British Prime Minister James Callaghan's 1976 speech to the Labour conference famously claimed that the option of state spending 'no longer exists'. It signalled a retreat all along the line:

The willingness of industry to invest in new plant and machinery requires, of course, that we overcome inflation, but also that industry is left with sufficient funds and has sufficient confidence to make new investments...I mean they must be able to make a surplus and that is a euphemism for saying they must be able to make a profit.

208 For a useful discussion of Reagan's victory written at the time, see Joanna Brenner and Robert Brenner, 'Reagan, the Right and the Working Class', *Verso Blogs*, 15 November 2016: https://www.versobooks.com/blogs/2939-reagan-the-right-and-the-working-class,Thatcher poll statistics from: https://www.ipsos.com/sites/default/files/migrations/en-uk/files/Assets/Docs/Polls/margaret-thatcher-poll-rating-trends.pdf

209 Joseph A. McCartin (2011) *Collision Course: Ronald Reagan, the air traffic controllers, and the strike that changed America*, Oxford University Press, Oxford, New York, p.74.

210 CNBC have produced a useful graph of data from the Bureau of Labour Services which illustrates this decline, at https://www.cnbc.com/2019/10/21/the-number-of-workers-on-strike-hits-the-highest-since-the-1980s.html

211 'Final Report of the Nationalised Industries Policy Group' (30 June 1977) Conservative Research Department, Economic Research Group, available at *Margaret Thatcher Foundation*, https://www.margaretthatcher.org/document/110795

212 The *Financial Times* commented the day after the biggest mass picket at Warrington, 'The police tactics at Warrington... show clearly they have learnt the lessons of mass picketing over the last ten years', *Financial Times*, 1 December 1983. Quoted in Audrey Farrell (1992) *Crime, Class and Corruption: The Politics of the Police*, Bookmarks, London, p.92.

213 Charles Moore (2005) *Margaret Thatcher: The Authorized Biography, Volume Two: Everything She Wants*, Allen Lane, London, p.2.

214 'The history of strikes in the UK' (September 12, 2015) *Office of National Statistics*. Available at: https://www.ons.gov.uk/employmentandlabourmarket/peopleinwork/employmentandemployeetypes/articles/thehistoryofstrikesin theuk/2015-09-21

215 Bill Crane (2017) 'The informal economy and India's working class: uneven and combined development', in *International Socialist Review*, Issue 106, Fall, 2017. Available at: https://isreview.org/issue/106/informal-economy-and-indias-working-class

216 Beverly J. Silver (2003) *Forces of Labor: Workers' Movements and Globalization since 1870*, Cambridge University Press, New York, p.127.

217 Beverly J. Silver (2003) *Forces of Labor: Worker's Movements and Globalization since 1870*, Cambridge University Press, New York, p.128.

218 For figures see Kim Moody (2012) 'Contextualizing Organized Labour in Expansion and Crisis: The Case of the US', in *Historical Materialism* 20, no. 1 (2012), pp.5–7.

219 Quoted in Joseph Choonara (2019) *Insecurity, Precarious Work and Labour Markets: Challenging the Orthodoxy*, Palgrave Macmillan, Switzerland, p.5.

220 Servaas Storm (May 14, 2020) 'The Economics and Politics of Social Democracy: A Reconsideration', *Institute for New Economic Thinking*. Available at: https://www.ineteconomics.

org/perspectives/blog/the-economics-and-politics-of-social-democracy-a-reconsideration

221 Neil Kinnock (1986) *Making Our Way*, Basil Blackwell, London, p.56.

222 Servaas Storm (May 14, 2020) 'The Economics and Politics of Social Democracy: A Reconsideration', *Institute for New Economic Thinking*. Available at: https://www.ineteconomics. org/perspectives/blog/the-economics-and-politics-of-social-democracy-a-reconsideration

223 Iain Dale, ed, (2007) *Labour Party General Election Manifestos*, Volume Two 1900-1997, Routledge, London, pp.343-82.

224 André Gorz (1980) *Farewell to the Working Class*, Pluto, London.

225 See for example Stuart Hall (1996) 'The Meaning of New Times', in Stuart Hall (1996) *Critical Dialogues in Cultural Studies*, Routledge, London, pp.223-37.

226 Their work has been influential in wider socialist circles, finding echoes for example in David Harvey's argument that 'the labour-capital contradiction...is not ...a primary contradiction to which all other contradictions are in some sense subservient'; David Harvey (2014) *Seventeen Contradictions and the End of Capitalism*, Oxford University, Oxford, p.68. For an extremely thorough examination of these arguments, see Raju Das (2017) *Marxist Class Theory for a Skeptical World*, Brill, Leiden, in particular, pp.70-3.

227 Michael Hardt and Toni Negri (2001) *Empire*, Harvard University Press, Cambridge.

228 Guy Standing (2014) *The Precariat: The New Dangerous Class*, Bloomsbury Academic, London.

229 Slavoj Žižek (2012) 'The Revolt of the Salaried Bourgeoisie' *London Review of Books* 34 (2): pp.9–10.

230 Manuel Castells (2009) *The Power of Identity*, Wiley-Blackwell, London.

231 International Labour Organisation (2013) *Key Indicators of*

the Labour Market, 8th ed. ILO, Geneva, available at: https://www.ilo.org/wcmsp5/groups/public/---dgreports/---stat/documents/publication/wcms_498929.pdf

232 Kim Moody (2017) *On New Terrain: How Capital Is Reshaping the Battleground of Class War*, Haymarket, Chicago, p.8.

233 Kim Moody (2017) *On New Terrain: How Capital Is Reshaping the Battleground of Class War*, Haymarket, Chicago, p.9.

234 Office of National Statistics (15 February 2022) 'UK Workforce jobs'. Available at: https://www.ons.gov.uk/employmentandlabourmarket/peopleinwork/employmentandemployeetypes/timeseries/jwr7/lms

235 *Fred Economic Research* has usefully tracked US Bureau of Labor's statistics. The data is presented here: https://fred.stlouisfed.org/graph/?graph_id=347814&rn=3405

236 Quoted in Moody (2017) *On New Terrain: How Capital Is Reshaping the Battleground of Class War*, Haymarket, Chicago, p.22.

237 Kevin Doogan has looked in detail at the evidence for the extent of offshoring and concludes amongst other things, 'there is a very limited sense in which mobile investment patterns can substantiate the idea of the ubiquity of capital flows, spatially indifferent and disembedded.' His conclusions can be found in Kevin Doogan (2009) *New Capitalism? The Transformation of Work*, Polity, Cambridge, pp.63-87.

238 Quoted in Charles Umney (2018) *Class Matters: Inequality and Exploitation in 21st Century Britain,* Pluto, London, p.48.

239 Paul Thompson (2005) 'Foundation and Empire: A Critique of Hardt and Negri', *Capital & Class* 29 (2), pp.84–6.

240 Joseph Choonara (2019) *Insecurity, Precarious Work and Labour Markets: Challenging the Orthodoxy,* Palgrave Macmillan, Switzerland, p.12.

241 Kim Moody (2017) *On New Terrain: How Capital Is Reshaping the Battleground of Class War*, Haymarket, Chicago, p.98.

242 'A Growing Sense of Inequity is Undermining Trust' (January 19 2020) *2020 Edelman Trust Barometer,* Edelman. Available at: https://www.edelman.com/trust/2020-trust-barometer

243 Charles Umney (2018) *Class Matters: Inequality and Exploitation in 21st Century Britain,* Pluto, London, p.57.

244 Robert MacDonald (2009) 'Precarious work: risk, choice and poverty traps', in Andy Furlong, ed, (2009) *Handbook of youth and adulthood,* Routledge, London, p.156.

245 Charles Umney (2018) *Class Matters: Inequality and Exploitation in 21st Century Britain,* Pluto, London, p.53.

246 Kim Moody (2017) *On New Terrain: How Capital Is Reshaping the Battleground of Class War,* Haymarket, Chicago, pp.47-48.

247 Beverly J. Silver (2003) *Forces of Labor: Worker's Movements and Globalization since 1870,* Cambridge University Press, New York, p.108.

248 Beverly J. Silver (2003) *Forces of Labor: Worker's Movements and Globalization since 1870,* Cambridge University Press, New York, p.107.

249 Kim Moody (2017) *On New Terrain: How Capital Is Reshaping the Battleground of Class War,* Haymarket, Chicago, p.109.

250 David Harvey (1999) *The Limits of Capital,* Verso, London, p.380.

251 Kim Moody (2017) *On New Terrain: How Capital Is Reshaping the Battleground of Class War,* Haymarket, Chicago, p.116.

252 Kim Moody (2017) *On New Terrain: How Capital Is Reshaping the Battleground of Class War,* Haymarket, Chicago, pp.74-5.

253 Max Roser (2017) 'Teachers and Professors', published online at *OurWorldInData.org.* Available here: 'https://ourworldindata.org/teachers-and-professors'.

254 Beverly J. Silver (2003) *Forces of Labor: Worker's Movements and Globalization since 1870,* Cambridge University Press, New York, p.115.

255 Beverly J. Silver (2003) *Forces of Labor: Worker's Movements and Globalization since 1870,* Cambridge University Press,

New York, p.115.

256 Andrew Van Dam (February 14, 2019) 'Teachers Strike Makes 2018 Biggest Year for Workers' Protest in Decades', *Washington Post*. Available at: https://www.washingtonpost.com/us-policy/2019/02/ 14/with-teachers-lead-more-worke rs-went-strike-than-any-year-since/ and Eric London (March 7, 2019) 'Teachers' Strike Wave Spreads Across Five Continents', *World Socialist Website*. Available at: https://www.wsws.org/en/articles/2019/03/07/teac-m07.html

257 Barra Roantree and Kartik Vira (2018) 'The rise and rise of women's employment in the UK', *Institute of Fiscal Studies*, IFS Briefing Note BN234, Available at: https://ifs.org.uk/uploads/BN234.pdf

258 Esteban Ortiz-Ospina, Sandra Tzvetkova and Max Roser (2018) 'Women's employment', published online at *OurWorldInData.org*. Available at: https://ourworldindata.org/female-labor-supply

259 Figures from Kim Moody (2017) *On New Terrain: How Capital Is Reshaping the Battleground of Class War*, Haymarket, Chicago, p.72.

260 Kim Moody (2017) *On New Terrain: How Capital Is Reshaping the Battleground of Class War*, Haymarket, Chicago, pp.64-5.

261 Mike Haynes (2011) 'Global cities, global workers in the 21st century', *International Socialism*, Issue: 132, Autumn 2011. Available at: http://isj.org.uk/issue-132/

262 Felix Richter (May 4, 2021) 'China Is the World's Manufacturing Superpower', *Statista*. Available at https://www.statista.com/chart/20858/top-10-countries-by-share-of-global-manufacturing-output/

263 Charles Duhigg and Keith Bradsher (January 21, 2012) 'How the US Lost Out on iPhone Work'. *New York Times*. https://www.nytimes.com/2012/01/22/business/apple-america-and-a-squeezed-middle-class.html

264 Parag Khanna (May 11, 2020) 'South-east Asia rides fourth

wave of regional growth', *Financial Times*. Available at: https://www.ft.com/content/c33e95f4-6acc-11ea-a6ac-9122541af204

265 Quoted in Mike Haynes (2011) 'Global cities, global workers in the 21st century', *International Socialism*, Issue: 132, Autumn 2011. Available at: http://isj.org.uk/issue-132/

266 Mike Davis (2017) *Planet of the Slums*, Vero, London, p.201.

267 For a full discussion of the relations between the 'informal' and 'formal' economies in the Global South, see See Raju Das (2017) *Marxist Class Theory for a Skeptical World,* Brill, Leiden, pp.361 and ff.

268 Immanuel Ness (2021) *Organizing Insurgency*, Pluto, London, p.37.

269 Leo Zeilig and David Seddon (2009) 'Introduction to the 2009 Edition: Resisting the Scramble for Africa', in Leo Zeilig, ed, (2009) *Class Struggle and Resistance*, Haymarket, Chicago, p.17.

270 Jeffrey R. Webber (2017), *The Last Day of Oppression and the First Day of the Same,* Pluto, London, p.14.

271 Jeffrey R. Webber (2017) *The Last Day of Oppression and the First Day of the Same,* Pluto, London, p.13.

272 Susan Spronk (2007) 'Roots of Resistance to Urban Water Privatization in Bolivia: The "New Working Class", the Crisis of Neoliberalism, and Public Services', *International Labor and Working-Class History* 71 *Spring 2007, p.20.*

273 Jeffrey Webber (2017) *The Last Day of Oppression and the First Day of the Same,* Pluto, London, p.15.

274 Mike Gonzalez (2005) 'Bolivia: The Rising of the People', *International Socialism* No 108, Autumn 2005, p.37.

275 Samni Zemni (2013), 'From Socio-economic Protest to National Revolt: The Labor Origins of the Tunisian Revolution', in Sami Zemni, Nouri Gana, eds, *The Making of the Tunisian Revolution,* Edinburgh University Press, Edinburgh, p.139.

276 Kasper Ly Netterstrom (2016) 'The Tunisian General Labor Union and the Advent of Democracy' *The Middle East Journal*

2016, Vol. 70, No. 3, p.387.

277 John Rees (2011) *The People Demand, A Short History of the Arab Revolutions,* Counterfire, London, p.62. See also Anne Alexander (2011) 'The Growing Social Soul of Egypt's Democratic Revolution', *International Socialism* No 131 (Summer), p.49.

278 John Rees (2011) *The People Demand, A Short History of the Arab Revolutions,* Counterfire, London, p.63.

279 Sameh Naguib (2021) 'The Tragedy of the Egyptian Revolution', in Colin Barker, Gareth Dale and Neil Davidson (2021) *Revolutionary Rehearsals in the Neoliberal Age,* Haymarket, Chicago, p.305.

280 'Unrest and economic underperformance haunt the emerging world' Editorial (July 31, 2021) *Economist.* Available at: https://www.economist.com/leaders/2021/07/31/unrest-and-economic-underperformance-stalk-the-emerging-world

281 'Civil Disobedience and General Strike-Field Report' (June 13, 2019) *Sudanese Professionals Association.* Available at: https://web.archive.org/web/20191218230923/https://www.sudaneseprofessionals.org/en/civil-disobedience-and-general-strike-field-report/

282 Muzan Alneel (January 23, 2021) 'Strategies and tactics in the Sudanese revolution' *Springmag.ca.* Available at: https://springmag.ca/strategies-and-tactics-in-the-sudanese-revolution

283 Muzan Alneel (January 23, 2001) 'Strategies and tactics in the Sudanese revolution'.

284 Thomas Piketty (2020) *Capital and Ideology,* Harvard University Press, London, p.423.

285 See Thomas Piketty (2020) *Capital and Ideology,* Harvard University Press, London, p.671.

286 Thomas Piketty (2020) *Capital and Ideology,* Harvard University Press, London, p.23.

287 Catherine Liu (2021) *Virtue Hoarders: The Case against the*

Professional Managerial Class, University of Minnesota Press, Minneapolis, p.9.

288 Pierre Dardot and Christian Laval (2009) *The New Way of the World: On Neoliberal Society,* London, Verso, p.4.

289 See the following, for example: John Gramlich (September 3, 2021) 'Majorities of Americans say unions have a positive effect on US and that decline in union membership is bad', *Pew Research Centre,* available at: https://www.pewresearch. org/fact-tank/2021/09/03/majorities-of-americans-say-unions-have-a-positive-effect-on-u-s-and-that-decline-in-union-membership-is-bad/ Kat Devlin and J.J. Moncus (August 6, 2020) 'Many around the world were pessimistic about inequality even before pandemic', *Pew Research Centre,* available here: https://www.pewresearch.org/fact-tank/2020/08/06/many-around-the-world-were-pessimistic-about-inequality-even-before-pandemic/ 'Little Public Support for Reductions in Federal Spending, Low trust in government; little confidence in the public's political wisdom' (April 11, 2019) *Pew Research Centre,* Available at: https://www.pewresearch.org/politics/2019/04/11/little-public-support-for-reductions-in-federal-spending/

290 Rahim Baizidi (2019) 'Paradoxical class: paradox of interest and political conservatism in the middle class', *Asian Journal of Political Science* 27:3, pp.272-85, and Liza G. Steele and Nate Breznau (2019) 'Attitudes toward Redistributive Policy: An Introduction', *MDPI,* available at https://www.mdpi.com/search?q=Attitudes+toward+Redistributive+Policy%3A+An+Introduction

291 John Curtice (1987) 'Interim Report: Party Politics' *The British Social Attitudes Survey 1987,* National Centre for Social Research, London, p.174.

292 Dr Kristian Niemietz (July 6, 2021) 'Left turn ahead: Surveying attitudes of young people towards capitalism and socialism', *Institute of Economic Affairs,* available at: https://

iea.org.uk/publications/left-turn-aheadsurveying-attitudes-of-young-people-towards-capitalism-and-socialism/

293 John Della Volpe (July 2016) 'The Millennial Agenda for the Next President. A Summary of Key Findings and Insights from the Harvard Public Opinion Project', *Harvard University Institute of Politics,* https://iop.harvard.edu/sites/default/files/content/docs/160718_Harvard%20IOP%20Poll%20Convention%20Summary.pdf

294 'A Growing Sense of Inequity is Undermining Trust' (January 19, 2020) *2020 Edelman Trust Barometer,* Edelman, available here: https://www.edelman.com/trust/2020-trust-barometer

295 Figure from Tony Cliff (1987) 'The working class and the oppressed', *Socialist Worker Review,* No. 101, (September). Available at: https://www.marxists.org/archive/cliff/works/1987/09/oppressed.html

296 Florence Sutcliffe-Braithwaite (2018) *Class, Politics and the Decline of Deference in England 1968-2000,* Oxford University Press, Oxford, pp.7-8.

297 For a discussion of this tendency see Manning Marable (1987) *African and Caribbean Politics,* Verso, London pp.150-1.

298 See Angela McRobbie (1996) *Looking Back at New Times and its Critics,* in Stuart Hall (1996) *Critical Dialogues in Cultural Studies,* Routledge, London, pp.230-61.

299 Georg Lukács (1971) *History and Class Consciousness,* Merlin, London, p.20.

300 Stephen Perkins (1993) *Marxism and the Proletariat. A Lukacsian Perspective,* Pluto, London p.161.

301 Georg Lukács (1971) *History and Class Consciousness,* Merlin, London, p.75.

302 Georg Lukács (1971) *History and Class Consciousness,* Merlin, London, p.310.

303 Alain Badiou is one of the influential left intellectuals who conceive of revolution as an unpredictable 'event' or 'break' beyond conventional understanding. The elitism and

unhelpfulness of this kind of thinking is explained well by Terry Eagleton in Terry Eagleton (2003) *Figures of Dissent,* Verso, London pp.246-53.

304 Georg Lukács (1971) *History and Class Consciousness,* Merlin, London, p.75.

305 Antonio Gramsci (1971) *Selections from the Prison Notebooks,* Lawrence and Wishart, London, pp.330-1.

306 Frederic Jameson (2003) 'Future City' *New Left Review* 21 (May/June), p.76.

307 Jonathan Marcus (July 8, 2017) 'Army Chief: Public has to understand why we need "boots on the ground"', *BBC.* Available at: https://www.bbc.co.uk/news/uk-40534771

308 For an excellent account of this dynamic, see Kevin Ovenden (2015) *Syriza: Inside the Labyrinth,* Verso, London, pp.42-64.

309 For an insight into the way the anti-austerity movement boosted Corbyn's leadership bid, see Alex Nunn (2016) *The Candidate: Jeremy Corbyn's Improbable Path to Power,* Verso, London, p.145.

310 See for example, Jane McAlevey (2014) *Raising Expectations (and Raising Hell) My Decade Fighting for the Labor Movement,* Verso, London. McAlevey is clearly right to be pointing out the importance of specifically workplace organising and insisting on doing it in the most inclusive, 'deepest' way possible. Her focus on the vulnerabilities of particular employers is valuable. Her approach, however, tends to be somewhat technical, and for all its emphasis on community, dangerously depoliticised. For a consideration of some of the issues raised see E. Tammy Kim, (May 5 2020) 'Structure Tests: How should unions organize in today's world?', *The Nation.* Available at: https://www.thenation.com/article/culture/jane-mcale vey-collective-bargain-book-review/

311 See for example, 'Jane McAlevey on how to Organize for Power', (April 21 2019) *Current Affairs.* Available at: https://www.currentaffairs.org/2019/04/jane-mcalevey-on-how-to-

organize-for-power

312 Asad Haider (2018) *Mistaken Identity*, Verso, London, p.24.

313 See Asad Haider (2018) *Mistaken Identity*, Verso, London, p.18.

314 Keeanga-Yamahtta Taylor (2016) *From #BlackLivesMatter to Black Liberation*, Haymarket, Chicago, p.80.

315 Catherine Liu (2021) *Virtue Hoarders: The Case against the Professional Managerial Class,* University of Minnesota Press, Minneapolis, p.8.

316 Georg Lukács (1971) *History and Class Consciousness*, Merlin, London, p.69.

317 Georg Lukács, (1970) *Lenin: A Study in the Unity of His Thought,* New Left Books, London, pp.31-2.

318 As Paul Krugman has put it 'my fiscal stimulus helps your economy, by increasing your exports – but you don't share in my addition to government debt', Paul Krugman (February 1, 2009) 'Protectionism and stimulus (wonkish)', *New York Times,* available at: https://krugman.blogs.nytimes.com/2009/02/01/protectionism-and-stimulus-wonkish/

319 Figures from the US Federal Bank, quoted in 'Out of Lockdown and Back into the Long Depression. An Interview with Michael Roberts' (July 6, 2021) *Spectre Journal,* available at: https://spectrejournal.com/out-of-lockdown-and-back-into-the-long-depression/

320 Antonio Gramsci (1971) *Selections from the Prison Notebooks,* Lawrence and Wishart, London, p.276.

CULTURE, SOCIETY & POLITICS

Contemporary culture has eliminated the concept and public figure of the intellectual. A cretinous anti-intellectualism presides, cheer-led by hacks in the pay of multinational corporations who reassure their bored readers that there is no need to rouse themselves from their stupor. Zer0 Books knows that another kind of discourse - intellectual without being academic, popular without being populist - is not only possible: it is already flourishing. Zer0 is convinced that in the unthinking, blandly consensual culture in which we live, critical and engaged theoretical reflection is more important than ever before.

If you have enjoyed this book, why not tell other readers by posting a review on your preferred book site.

You may also wish to
subscribe to our Zer0 Books YouTube Channel.

Rebel Rebel
Chris O'Leary
David Bowie: every single song. Everything you want to know, everything you didn't know.
Paperback: 978-1-78099-244-0 ebook: 978-1-78099-713-1

Cartographies of the Absolute
Alberto Toscano, Jeff Kinkle
An aesthetics of the economy for the twenty-first century.
Paperback: 978-1-78099-275-4 ebook: 978-1-78279-973-3

Malign Velocities
Accelerationism and Capitalism
Benjamin Noys
Long listed for the Bread and Roses Prize 2015, *Malign Velocities* argues against the need for speed, tracking acceleration as the symptom of the ongoing crises of capitalism.
Paperback: 978-1-78279-300-7 ebook: 978-1-78279-299-4

Babbling Corpse
Vaporwave and the Commodification of Ghosts
Grafton Tanner
Paperback: 978-1-78279-759-3 ebook: 978-1-78279-760-9

New Work New Culture
Work we want and a culture that strengthens us
Frithjof Bergmann
A serious alternative for mankind and the planet.
Paperback: 978-1-78904-064-7 ebook: 978-1-78904-065-4

Romeo and Juliet in Palestine
Teaching Under Occupation
Tom Sperlinger
Life in the West Bank, the nature of pedagogy and the role of a university under occupation.
Paperback: 978-1-78279-637-4 ebook: 978-1-78279-636-7

Color, Facture, Art and Design
Iona Singh
This materialist definition of fine-art develops guidelines for architecture, design, cultural-studies and ultimately social change.
Paperback: 978-1-78099-629-5 ebook: 978-1-78099-630-1

Sweetening the Pill
or How We Got Hooked on Hormonal Birth Control
Holly Grigg-Spall
Has contraception liberated or oppressed women?
Sweetening the Pill breaks the silence on the dark side of hormonal contraception.
Paperback: 978-1-78099-607-3 ebook: 978-1-78099-608-0

Why Are We The Good Guys?
Reclaiming Your Mind from the Delusions of Propaganda
David Cromwell
A provocative challenge to the standard ideology that Western power is a benevolent force in the world.
Paperback: 978-1-78099-365-2 ebook: 978-1-78099-366-9

The Writing on the Wall
On the Decomposition of Capitalism and its Critics
Anselm Jappe, Alastair Hemmens
A new approach to the meaning of social emancipation.
Paperback: 978-1-78535-581-3 ebook: 978-1-78535-582-0

Neglected or Misunderstood
The Radical Feminism of Shulamith Firestone
Victoria Margree
An interrogation of issues surrounding gender, biology,
sexuality, work and technology, and the ways in which our
imaginations continue to be in thrall to ideologies of maternity
and the nuclear family.
Paperback: 978-1-78535-539-4 ebook: 978-1-78535-540-0

How to Dismantle the NHS in 10 Easy Steps
(Second Edition)
Youssef El-Gingihy
The story of how your NHS was sold off and why you will
have to buy private health insurance soon. A new expanded
second edition with chapters on junior doctors' strikes and
government blueprints for US-style healthcare.
Paperback: 978-1-78904-178-1 ebook: 978-1-78904-179-8

Digesting Recipes
The Art of Culinary Notation
Susannah Worth
A recipe is an instruction, the imperative tone of the expert,
but this constraint can offer its own kind of potential. A recipe
need not be a domestic trap but might instead offer escape –
something to fantasise about or aspire to.
Paperback: 978-1-78279-860-6 ebook: 978-1-78279-859-0

Most titles are published in paperback and as an ebook.
Paperbacks are available in traditional bookshops. Both print
and ebook formats are available online.
Follow us at: https://www.facebook.com/ZeroBooks https://
twitter.com/Zer0Books https://www.instagram.com/zero.books